AMERICA

STUDY GUIDE

VOLUME I / BRIEF SIXTH EDITION

AMERICA

A NARRATIVE HISTORY

TINDALL and SHI

STUDY GUIDE

VOLUME I / BRIEF SIXTH EDITION

CHARLES W. EAGLES
UNIVERSITY OF MISSISSIPPI

W · W · NORTON & COMPANY · NEW YORK · LONDON

Composition and layout by Roberta Flechner Graphics.

ISBN 0-393-92505-6 (pbk.)

W.W. Norton & Company, Inc.
500 Fifth Avenue, New York, N.Y. 10110
www.wwnorton.com

W. W. Norton & Company Ltd.
Castle House, 75/76 Wells Street, London W1T 3QT

1 2 3 4 5 6 7 8 9 0

CONTENTS

INTRODUCTION

This *Study Guide* is designed to help you learn the important concepts in *America: A Narrative History,* Brief Sixth Edition, by George B. Tindall and David E. Shi. It is not intended as a replacement for the textbook, but as an aid to be used along with the text. When used conscientiously, this *Study Guide* will help you to understand the major themes in American history and to do well on quizzes based on your reading.

STRUCTURE OF THIS STUDY GUIDE

Each chapter of the *Study Guide* contains the following sections:

Chapter Objectives
Chapter Outline
Key Items of Chronology
Terms to Master
Vocabulary Building
Exercises for Understanding:
    Multiple-Choice Questions
    True-False Questions
    Essay Questions

The purpose of each of the sections, along with the instructions for its use, is explained below.

Chapter Objectives

For each chapter you will find about five objectives, or key concepts, on which you should focus your attention as you read. You should read the whole of each chapter, taking in details as well as major themes, but by keeping the chapter objectives in mind, you will avoid getting bogged down and missing the key ideas.

Chapter Outline

Skim this outline carefully before you begin reading a chapter. The outline provides a more detailed overview than do the objectives. Often headings in the outline are worded to suggest questions about the material. For example, "Duties of the King" and "patterns of Colonization" raise the questions "What were the duties of the king?" and "What were the patterns of colonization?" Look for the answers to such questions as you read the text. This approach will help those of you who are new to reading history.

Key Items of Chronology

Each chapter of this *Study Guide* will include a list of dates. You need not learn every date you encounter in the chapter, but if you learn the key ones listed here and any other dates emphasized by your instructor, you will have the sound chronological framework so important for understanding historical events.

Keep in mind that dates, while important, are not the sole subject matter of history. Seldom will any of the quizzes in this *Study Guide* ask for recall of dates. On the other hand, term papers and answers to essay questions should include important dates and show that you are familiar with the chronology of your subject.

Terms to Master

This section of the *Study Guide* gives you a list of important terms to study. (Remember, of course, that your instructor may emphasize additional terms that you should learn.) After reading each chapter, return to the list of terms and write a brief definition of each. If you cannot recall the term readily, turn to the relevant pages in the textbook and reread the discussion of the term. If you need or want to consult another source, go to the annotated bibliography at the end of the relevant chapter, or ask your instructor for suggestions.

Vocabulary Building

This is a section of the *Study Guide* that you may or may not need. If you do not know the meaning of the words or terms listed in Vocabulary Building, look them up in a dictionary before you begin reading a chapter. By looking up such words and then using them yourself, you will increase your vocabulary.

When the terms in Vocabulary Building are not readily found in the standard dictionary or when their use in your text lends them a special meaning, we have defined them for you. We've used the *American Heritage Dictionary,* Second College Edition, as a guide to determine which terms should be defined here for you.

Exercises for Understanding

You should reserve these exercises to use as a check on your reading after you study the chapter. The multiple-choice and true-false questions included here will test your recall and understanding of the facts in the chapter. The answers to these questions are found at the end of each *Study Guide* chapter.

Essay Questions

The essay questions that come next may be used in several ways. If you are using this *Study Guide* entirely on your own, you should try to outline answers to these questions based on your reading of the chapter. In the early stages of the course you may want to consider writing formal answers to these essay questions just as you would if you encountered them on an exam. The questions will often be quite broad and will lead you to think about material in the chapter in different ways. By reviewing the essay questions in this *Study Guide* before attending class, you will better understand the class lecture or discussion.

STUDYING HISTORY

The term "history" has been defined in many ways. One way to define it is "everything that has happened in the past." But there are serious problems with this definition. First, it is simply impossible to recount *everything* that has happened in the past. Any single event is a combination of an infinite number of subevents. Each of these is itself composed of an unlimited number of subevents. The past, which includes everything that has happened, is shapeless; history is a way of lending shape to the past by focusing on significant events and their relationships.

Second, the historical record is limited. As you will discover, there is much we don't know about everyday life in seventeenth-century America. History must be based on fact and evidence. The historian then, using the evidence available, fashions a story in which certain past events are connected and take on special meaning or significance. If we accept this definition, we will recognize that much history is subjective, or influenced by the perspective and bias of the historian attempting to give meaning to events.

This is why there is so much disagreement about the importance of some past events. You may have been taught in high school that it was important simply to learn dates and facts: that the Declaration of Independence was adopted on July 4, 1776, or that Franklin Roosevelt was inaugurated on March 4, 1933. But these facts by themselves are limited in meaning. They gain significance when they become parts of larger stories, such as why the American colonies revolted against England, or how America responded to the Great Depression. When historians construct stories or narratives in which these facts or events take on special significance, room for disagreement creeps in.

Since it is valid for historians to disagree, you should not automatically accept what any one historian writes. You should learn to apply general rules of logic and evidence in assessing the validity of different historical interpretations. This *Study Guide* will at times give you an opportunity to assess different interpretations of events. By doing this, you will learn to question what you read and hear, to think critically.

HOW TO READ A TEXTBOOK

Reading a textbook should be both pleasurable and profitable. The responsibility for this is partly the author's and partly yours, the reader's. George Tindall and David Shi have written a text that should teach and entertain. In order to get the most out of it, you must read actively and critically. One way to avoid passive, mindless reading is to write, underline, or highlight material by hand. Simply by highlighting or underlining pertinent passages in the textbook, you will later be better able to recall what you have read, and will be able to review important material quickly. The key to effective highlighting is to be judicious about what you choose to mark. You should highlight key words and phrases, not whole sentences unless all the words are important. For example, the two paragraphs below show the way we would highlight them:

> Even the Tudors, who acted as autocrats, preserved the forms of constitutional procedure. In the making of laws the king's subjects consented through representatives in the House of Commons. By custom and practice **the principle was established that the king taxed his subjects only with the consent of Parliament.** And by its control of the purse strings Parliament would draw other strands of power into its hands. This structure of habit broadened down from precedent to precedent to form a **constitution that was** not written in one place, or for that matter, **not fully written down at all.** The *Magna Carta* (Great Charter) of 1215, for instance, had been a statement of privileges wrested by certain nobles from the king, but it became part of a broader tradition that the people as a whole had rights which even the king could not violate.

> **A further buttress to English liberty** was the **great body of common law,** which had developed since the twelfth century in royal courts established to

check the arbitrary caprice of local nobles. Without laws to cover every detail, judges had to exercise their own ideas of fairness in settling disputes. **Decisions once made became precedents for later decisions** and over the years a body of judge-made law developed, the outgrowth more of experience than of abstract logic. Through the courts the principle evolved that **a subject could be arrested or his goods seized only upon a warrant issued by a court,** and that **he was entitled to a trial by a jury of his peers** (his equals) in accordance with established rules of evidence.

Probably no two people would agree on exactly which words in the passage should be underlined, but you can readily see that we have emphasized only the major points concerning English justice.

Highlighting like this can be helpful, but even more useful in increasing your retention of the material is jotting down brief notes about what you read. For example, from the passage above you might list some key elements in the development of liberty under the Tudors: the principle that the king could tax his subjects only with the consent of Parliament, the development of an unwritten constitution, the principle that a court order was required for arrest or seizure of property, and the principle of trial by jury.

Taking notes makes it easier to commit important points to memory. This will be particularly helpful when you review for a test.

ACKNOWLEDGMENTS

I wish to thank George B. Tindall and David E. Shi for having written the excellent text around which I developed this *Study Guide*. My hope is that the text and the *Study Guide* will combine to promote in students a clear understanding of the history of the United States. I have a great debt to Steven Forman and Matthew Arnold, my editors at W. W. Norton & Company, and Steve's assistant, Sarah England, who have again used their considerable skill to fashion the final product.

C.W.E.

1

THE COLLISION OF CULTURES

CHAPTER OBJECTIVES

After you finish reading and studying this chapter, you should be able to

1. Describe and explain the cultural and biological exchanges that occurred between Europe and America following the discovery of the New World.

2. Explain the different characteristics of the European contacts with the New World before the permanent settlements of the seventeenth century.

3. Assess the strengths of the European nations compared to the Indian cultures in the New World.

4. Appreciate the characteristics of the Spanish-controlled southwestern United States.

5. Understand the rivalries among European countries for influence in the New World.

CHAPTER OUTLINE

I. Indian cultures before Columbus
   A. Varieties in the Americas
   B. North American Indian life
      1. Characteristics
         a. Smaller tribes
         b. Migratory
         c. Communal lands
         d. Village life in Ohio and Mississippi River valleys
      2. Response to European invasion
         a. Weaknesses

      b. Resistance

      c. Ability to adapt

II. First European contacts with the New World

  A. Rise of "modern" Europe

    1. Growth in learning

    2. Development of towns, trade, and corporations

    3. Rise of nation states

    4. Protestant Reformation

  B. Appeal of Asia

  C. Voyages of Columbus

    1. Background

    2. Expedition of 1492

    3. Later voyages

  D. Amerigo Vespucci

  E. Biological exchanges

    1. Animals

    2. Plants

    3. Devices

    4. Diseases

III. Exploration and conquest of the New World

  A. English, Portuguese, and others

    1. John Cabot

    2. Brazil

    3. Spanish dominance

  B. Creation of the Spanish empire

    1. Spanish avantages

      a. Technological

      b. Cultural

    2. Conquistadors

      a. Hernan Cortés

      b. Francisco Pizarro

  C. *Encomienda* system

    1. Structure

      a. Affluent Europeans

      b. Subject natives

    2. Role of Catholic missionaries

    3. Spanish heritage

      a. Spanish names

      b. Catholicism

      c. "Spanish borderlands"

        i. Ponce de León

        ii. Protection

D. Spanish Southwest
 1. Impact of the church
 2. New Mexico
  a. Juan de Oñate
  b. Indian revolt
  c. Royal province
E. Spain's rivals in North America
 1. The French
  a. Explorers
   i. Verrazano
   ii. Cartier
   iii. Champlain
   iv. Joliet and Marquette
  b. Canada
  c. New Orleans
 2. The Dutch privateers
 3. British defeat of the Spanish Armada

KEY ITEMS OF CHRONOLOGY

Crossing from Siberia to Alaska	12,000 B.C.
Columbus's first voyage to the New World	1492
John Cabot sailed to North America	1497
Amerigo Vespucci sailed to the New World	1499
First African slaves imported to the West Indies	1503
Ponce de León's exploration of Florida	1513
Cortés invaded Mexico	1519
Voyage of Verrazano	1524
Cartier established colony near Quebec	1542
British defeated Spanish Armada	1588
Mexico became a royal province	1608
Joliet and Marquette journeyed down the Mississippi River	1673

TERMS TO MASTER

Listed below are some important people or terms with which you should be familiar after your study of the chapter. Identify each name or term.

1. Christopher Columbus
2. San Salvador
3. Amerigo Vespucci
4. biological exchange
5. John Cabot
6. Hernan Cortés
7. Tenochtitlán
8. conquistadors
9. Francisco Pizarro
10. *encomienda*
11. Spanish borderlands
12. Juan Ponce de León
13. *presidio*
14. New Mexico
15. Juan de Oñate
16. Giovanni da Verrazano
17. Jacques Cartier
18. Spanish Armada

VOCABULARY BUILDING

Listed below are some words or phrases used in this chapter. Look in the dictionary for the meaning of each term you do not know.

1. recede
2. forage
3. monumental
4. zeal
5. amok
6. diffusion
7. hemisphere
8. ecological
9. complementary
10. landfall
11. preserve (n.)
12. subjugation
13. impregnable
14. remnant
15. tribute
16. extinct
17. riven
18. mythic
19. lucrative
20. enmity

EXERCISES FOR UNDERSTANDING

When you have finished reading the chapter, answer each of the following questions. If you have difficulty, go back to the text and reread the section of the chapter related to the question.

Multiple-Choice Questions

Select the letter of the choice that best completes the statement.

1. Recent archaeological evidence suggests that people first arrived in the New World
   A. 5,000 years ago.
   B. 10,000 years ago.
   C. 15,000 years ago.
   D. more than 15,000 years ago.

2. The most culturally sophisticated Indian culture in the New World was the
   A. Aztec or Mayan.
   B. Pueblo or Creek.
   C. Iroquois.
   D. Cherokee.

3. The most significant attraction that prompted Europeans to sail toward the New World was the
   A. fountain of youth.
   B. riches of Asia.
   C. possibility of enslaving Indians.
   D. coffee plantations of Brazil.

4. One of Columbus's major goals in his voyages was to
   A. prove the world was round.
   B. reach Asia by sailing east.
   C. enslave Indians.
   D. find gold and riches.

5. America was named for
   A. Columbus's daughter.
   B. Vespucci.
   C. the queen of Spain.
   D. the god of discovery.

6. Smallpox and typhus
   A. killed many Europeans in the New World.
   B. killed many animals brought to America.
   C. devastated Indian populations.
   D. all of the above

7. Tenochtitlán was
    A. Cortés's Indian guide.
    B. an island discovered by Pizarro.
    C. the capital of the Aztec empire.
    D. the language spoken by most Indians.

8. European diets were revolutionized when the following were adopted from the New World:
    A. pigs and chickens.
    B. corn and potatoes.
    C. wheat and coffee.
    D. all of the above

9. Most of the early Spanish settlements and explorations in North America were made
    A. in the East Coast states.
    B. in the Southwest.
    C. in South Carolina.
    D. along the Mississippi River.

10. English colonization of America was encouraged by
    A. Mary, Queen of Scots.
    B. the discovery of gold in New Mexico.
    C. Cortés's victory at Vera Cruz.
    D. the defeat of the Spanish Armada.

True-False Questions

Indicate whether each statement is true or false.

1. In 1492 Columbus believed that he had reached Asia.

2. Europeans brought pigs, cattle, and sheep to the New World.

3. The game of lacrosse had English origins.

4. The first European to see the North American continent was Hernan Cortés.

5. Weaknesses of Indians in Mexico included the lack of iron and horses.

6. Capitalism was the key to successful colonial development.

7. The Protestant Church played a major role in the Spanish borderlands.

8. The Spanish used religion as a primary means to control their colonies.

9. The French had a monopoly on colonies in the New World throughout the 1500s.

10. The Spanish founded New Orleans early in the seventeenth century.

Essay Questions

1. How did the Spanish interaction with Native Americans differ from the way English settlers dealt with Indians?

2. Describe and evaluate the significance of the biological interchange between the Old and New Worlds. Which group did it affect more, Europeans or Indians?

3. How did the Spanish extend their influence in the New World? How extensive was their empire?

4. Explain how other nations challenged Spanish dominance. Which was the most successful?

5. What long term effects did the Spanish have on the New World?

ANSWERS TO MULTIPLE-CHOICE AND TRUE-FALSE QUESTIONS

Multiple-Choice Questions

1-D, 2-A, 3-B, 4-D, 5-B, 6-C, 7-C, 8-B, 9-B, 10-D

True-False Questions

1-T, 2-T, 3-F, 4-F, 5-T, 6-T, 7-F, 8-T, 9-F, 10-F

2

ENGLAND AND ITS COLONIES

CHAPTER OBJECTIVES

After you finish reading and studying this chapter, you should be able to

1. Identify the key features in the settlement and early development of each of the thirteen North American colonies of England, particularly Virginia, Massachusetts, Maryland, and New York.

2. Understand the chief features of English colonization in North America as a whole.

3. Compare and contrast English colonization efforts with those of Spain and France.

4. Assess the relations between the settlers of the thirteen colonies and the Indians.

5. Appreciate the different motives involved in the settlement of the colonies.

6. Evaluate the success of the English colonies.

CHAPTER OUTLINE

I. English explorations and colonies
   A. Roanoke
   B. Diversity of colonies
   C. Compared to the Spanish colonies

II. The Chesapeake
   A. Virginia
      1. Settlement of Jamestown
      2. John Smith

   3. Relations with Indians
   4. Reforms after 1618
   5. Tobacco trade
   6. Made a royal colony
  B. Maryland
   1. The Calverts
   2. Catholicism
  C. New England
   1. Early settlers
    a. Middle-class families
    b. Healthy
    c. Puritans
   2. Pilgrims at Plymouth Colony
    a. Separatists
    b. William Bradford
    c. Mayflower Compact
   3. Massachusetts Bay
    a. Non-Separating Congregationalists
    b. John Winthrop
    c. "City upon a hill"
    d. Provincial government
   4. Rhode Island
    a. Roger Williams
     i. Banishment
     ii. Providence
    b. Anne Hutchinson
     i. Provocative beliefs
     ii. Trial
     iii. Banishment
   5. Connecticut, New Hampshire, and Maine
   6. Indian relations
    a. English seek to subordinate Indians
    b. Initial relations
    c. Pequot War of 1637
    d. Peaceful fur trade
    e. King Philip's War of 1675

III. Settlements after 1660
  A. The English Civil War
  B. Southern colonies
   1. The Carolinas
    a. Albemarle
    b. Lord Ashley-Cooper
   2. Indian relations
    a. Deerskin trade

        b. Diseases
        c. Wars and revolts
    C. Middle Colonies
       1. New York
          a. Dutch origin
          b. Conquest by English
          c. The Iroquois
             i. Indian unity
            ii. Fights for hunting grounds
           iii. Conflicts with French
           iv. Neutrality between French and English
       2. New Jersey
       3. Pennsylvania and Delaware
          a. Quakers
          b. William Penn
    D. Georgia
       1. James Oglethorpe
       2. Royal colony

IV. English colonial success
    A. Attractions
    B. Advantages

KEY ITEMS OF CHRONOLOGY

Sir Walter Raleigh's expedition to America	1584
Settlement of Jamestown	1607
First meeting of General Assembly of Virginia	1619
First Africans imported to Virginia	1619
Mayflower Compact	1620
Plymouth settled	1620
Virginia became a royal colony	1624
Massachusetts Bay settled	1630
Maryland first settled	1634
Roger Williams founded Providence, Rhode Island	1636
Pequot War	1637
English Civil War	1642–1649
Restoration of monarchy	1660
Carolinas settled	1670
King Philip's War	1675
Pennsylvania founded	1681
Yamasee War	1715–1717
South Carolina became a royal colony	1719
Georgia established	1733

TERMS TO MASTER

Listed below are some important people or terms with which you should be familiar after your study of the chapter. Identify each name or term.

1. Sir Walter Raleigh
2. Virginia Dare
3. "lost colonists"
4. the Stuarts
5. Chesapeake Bay
6. Jamestown
7. Captain John Smith
8. Pocahontas
9. headright policy
10. indentured servant
11. Pilgrims
12. *Mayflower*
13. Mayflower Compact
14. Non-Separating Congregationalists
15. Roger Williams
16. Anne Hutchinson
17. Pequot War
18. proprietary colony
19. Lord Ashley-Cooper
20. patroon
21. Iroquois
22. Quakers
23. William Penn

VOCABULARY BUILDING

Listed below are some words or phrases used in this chapter. Look in the dictionary for the meaning of each term you do not know.

1. pillage
2. dynasty
3. turbulent
4. trademark
5. autocratic
6. pale (n.)
7. subjugate
8. marauding
9. thatched
10. swashbuckling
11. noxious
12. plunder
13. decimate
14. asylum
15. proviso
16. stipulate
17. unregenerate
18. deluded
19. arduous
20. reciprocity
21. cumbersome
22. matrilineal
23. voracious
24. infighting
25. vernacular
26. flounder (v.)

EXERCISES FOR UNDERSTANDING

When you have finished reading the chapter, answer each of the following questions. If you have difficulty, go back to the text and reread the section of the chapter related to the question.

Multiple-Choice Questions

Select the letter of the choice that best completes the statement.

1. The unsuccessful English colony known as the "lost colony" was in
   A. Virginia.
   B. Massachusetts.
   C. North Carolina.
   D. New Jersey.

2. Compared to Spanish colonization, English colonization
   A. was more autocratic.
   B. involved conquering more Indians.
   C. placed greater stress on planting settlements.
   D. all of the above

3. Captain John Smith was a leader in
   A. Virginia.
   B. Massachusetts Bay.
   C. Plymouth.
   D. Georgia.

4. Maryland, the first proprietary colony, was unusual because it was
   A. controlled by a group of businessmen.
   B. started as a philanthropic experiment.
   C. a refuge for Catholics.
   D. primarily a military outpost.

5. The effort to establish new colonies in America was largely suspended by the English during the
   A. civil war and Cromwell's Puritan dictatorship.
   B. time James I was on the British throne.
   C. Restoration reign of Charles II.
   D. reign of Queen Elizabeth I.

6. Compared to the Chesapeake colonies, the New England colonies had
   A. a stronger planter elite.
   B. fewer women.
   C. a longer life expectancy.
   D. fewer colonists in the seventeenth century.

7. The English colonies were organized by
   A. the English army.
   B. the Anglican Church.
   C. Parliament.
   D. joint-stock companies.

8. Non-Separating Congregationalists settled in
   A. Massachusetts Bay.
   B. Pennsylvania.
   C. Plymouth.
   D. Maryland.

9. The settlement of North Carolina was notable for
   A. a plan for a feudal-like system of land ownership.
   B. religious toleration that even extended to Jews.
   C. early domination of the colony by people from Barbados.
   D. all of the above

10. The English colonists' general strategy for dealing with Indians in New England stressed
    A. subordination of Indians to gain their land.
    B. exploitation of the fur trade through trading posts.
    C. conversion of Indians to Christianity.
    D. treaties for amicable and stable relations.

True-False Questions

Indicate whether each statement is true or false.

1. The English patterned their settlements in America after their experience in Ireland.

2. The "headright" policy in Virginia determined the distribution of land.

3. The *Mayflower* brought settlers to Plymouth.

4. Pequot successfully united the Iroquois in New York.

5. John Winthrop was a leader of Rhode Island.

6. New York was originally settled by the French Huguenots.

7. Anne Hutchinson angered Puritan leaders by claiming that most ministers were preaching salvation by good works rather than by God's grace.

8. The "inner light" doctrine motivated many settlers in New Jersey.

9. Georgia was a philanthropic experiment in prison reform.

10. By 1650, the average person in the English colonies was better fed, clothed, and housed than his counterpart in Britain.

Essay Questions

1. The English colonies displayed significant diversity. When compared to the Spanish, French, and Dutch settlements, however, what characteristics did the English colonies have in common with those settlements?

2. How was religion important in the settlement of the English colonies?

3. Which two English colonies were most *unlike* one another? Describe their differences.

4. Explain the importance of Indian relations to the colonies.

5. Compare and contrast Virginia and Massachusetts Bay with regard to motivations for colonization, land systems, religious practices, and general success as colonies. Make a similar analysis for Rhode Island and Pennsylvania.

ANSWERS TO MULTIPLE-CHOICE AND TRUE-FALSE QUESTIONS

Multiple-Choice Questions

1-C, 2-C, 3-A, 4-C, 5-A, 6-C, 7-D, 8-A, 9-D, 10-A

True-False Questions

1-T, 2-T, 3-T, 4-F, 5-F, 6-F, 7-T, 8-F, 9-T, 10-T

3

COLONIAL WAYS OF LIFE

CHAPTER OBJECTIVES

After you finish reading and studying this chapter, you should be able to

1. Identify population patterns in the colonies and explain their impact on institutions and the development of the colonies.

2. Identify and compare the chief features of the Southern, New England, and Middle colonies.

3. Explain the land and labor systems developed in the colonies, the reasons for their development, and their long-range influences on the colonies.

4. Describe the major features of social life in the colonies in the seventeenth and eighteenth centuries.

5. Explain the effects of the Enlightenment and the Great Awakening on the colonies.

CHAPTER OUTLINE

I. The people and environment of early America
   A. Sources of immigration
   B. British migrants
      1. Four streams
      2. Folkways
   C. Seaboard environment
      1. Indian attitudes toward environment
      2. European ideas of land ownership
      3. Environmental changes

    D. Demographic developments
       1. Population growth
       2. High birthrate
       3. Low death rate
    E. Women in colonies
       1. Assumed inferiority
       2. Work
          a. Domestic sphere
          b. Greater opportunities
       3. Short supply

II. The economy and society of the southern colonies
    A. Agriculture
       1. Important crops
       2. Nature of the headright system
       3. Growth of large-scale farming
    B. Labor
       1. System of indentured servants
       2. Slavery
          a. Need for slavery
          b. African roots
             i. Differences and similarities
             ii. West African society
          c. Atlantic creoles
          d. Demand for slaves

III. New England colonial life
    A. Land policy of the towns
    B. Homes and family life
    C. The economy and commerce
       1. Farming
       2. Fishing
       3. Trade
          a. Balance of trade problem
          b. Shortage of hard money
    D. Puritan religion
       1. Attitudes toward clothing, drink, and sex
       2. Relationship to the Church of England
       3. Elements of democracy in the church
       4. The covenant theory
       5. Cohesiveness of Puritan society
    E. Strains within the Puritan consensus
       1. Relations of parents and sons
       2. Effects of individual accountability to God
       3. Development of the Half-Way Covenant

      4. Witchcraft hysteria in Salem
        a. Social conflicts in Salem
        b. Events of 1692
        c. Explanation of hysteria

IV. The middle colonies
    A. Influences of New England and the South
      1. Crops and commerce
      2. Land policies
    B. Ethnic mix
      1. Quakers
      2. Germans
      3. Scotch-Irish

V. Colonial cities
    A. Population
      1. Five major ports
      2. Classes
    B. Urban problems
    C. The urban web
      1. Transportation
      2. Postal service
      3. Newspapers

VI. Intellectual trends
    A. The Enlightenment
      1. Impact of scientific revolution
      2. Effects on established beliefs
    B. The American Enlightenment and Benjamin Franklin
    C. Education in the colonies
    D. The Great Awakening
      1. Causes of the religious revival
      2. Roles of Edwards and Whitefield
      3. Scope of the revival movement
      4. Effects of the Great Awakening

KEY ITEMS OF CHRONOLOGY

First blacks arrive at Jamestown	1619
Founding of Harvard College	1636
Half-Way Covenant accepted	1662
Newton's theory of gravity	1687
Witchcraft hysteria at Salem	1692
Trial of John Peter Zenger	1735

Great Awakening   1730s–1740s
Jonathan Edwards's sermon
    "Sinners in the Hands of an Angry God"   1741

TERMS TO MASTER

Listed below are some important people or terms with which you should be familiar after your study of the chapter. Identify each name or term.

1. headright
2. indentured servant
3. staple crop
4. American creole
5. balance of trade
6. "invisible" charges
7. "triangular trade"
8. covenant theory
9. Half-Way Covenant
10. Scotch-Irish
11. John Peter Zenger
12. Deists
13. John Locke
14. Benjamin Franklin
15. Jonathan Edwards
16. George Whitefield

VOCABULARY BUILDING

Listed below are some words or phrases used in this chapter. Look in the dictionary for the meaning of each term you do not know.

1. clannish
2. forage
3. decimate
4. induce
5. husbandry
6. fluid (adj.)
7. clapboard
8. preclude
9. barter
10. covenant
11. theocracy
12. magistrate
13. recant
14. frenetic
15. salient
16. curmudgeon
17. pluralism
18. piety
19. licentiousness
20. mesmerize

EXERCISES FOR UNDERSTANDING

When you have finished reading the chapter, answer each of the following questions. If you have difficulty, go back to the text and reread the section of the chapter related to the question.

Multiple-Choice Questions

Select the letter of the choice that best completes the statement.

1. Most migrants to America were
   A. males under twenty-five years old.
   B. indentured servants.
   C. slaves.
   D. wealthy.

2. Compared to Native Americans, European colonists
   A. had fewer domestic animals.
   B. practiced more subsistence farming.
   C. were not as migratory.
   D. all of the above

3. Women in the English colonies
   A. were entirely restricted to domestic work.
   B. found new occupations because of a labor shortage.
   C. dominated the clergy in the Great Awakening.
   D. voted and held public offices.

4. Distinctive features of the southern economy included
   A. its climate.
   B. a market in England for its staple products.
   C. large-scale production.
   D. all of the above

5. Indentured servants
   A. always came to the American colonies voluntarily.
   B. worked in exchange for transportation to America.
   C. came in family groups.
   D. were just like slaves.

6. In general the Puritans
   A. refused to enjoy sensuous delight in the world.
   B. were total abstainers from alcoholic beverages.
   C. believed that the things of the world were made by God to be enjoyed by man.
   D. wore dark-colored clothes to emphasize their denial of physical pleasures.

7. The witchcraft hysteria in the 1690s was probably caused by
   A. the Great Awakening.
   B. social strains in the Massachusetts colony.
   C. dietary insufficiencies among young women.
   D. the horrors of the "Middle Passage."

8. Two essential elements of the colonial New England economy were
   A. fishing and shipping.
   B. slavery and plantations.
   C. staple crops for export and ships to carry them.
   D. hard money to invest and manufacturing.

9. The greatest ethnic diversity existed in
   A. New England.
   B. the Middle colonies.
   C. the Southern colonies.
   D. the Chesapeake area.

10. In the Great Awakening of the 1730s and 1740s,
    A. Jonathan Edwards advocated Deism.
    B. colonists returned to the church in large numbers except in the Middle colonies.
    C. new religious groups helped undermine state-supported churches.
    D. Charles Chauncey and Jonathan Mayhew played key roles in Boston.

True-False Questions

Indicate whether each statement is true or false.

1. The birthrate was lower in the colonies than in England.

2. The headright system was used in New England.

3. In the eighteenth century, nearly all slaves came to the colonies from Brazil and the Caribbean.

4. The absence of the Anglican bishop in the colonies resulted in greater conformity to rules among the churches.

5. As a result of the Great Awakening, many of the religious denominations formed new colleges.

6. Merchants were the primary members of the upper class in colonial towns.

7. The Scotch-Irish usually settled in colonial cities.

8. The jury in the John Peter Zenger trial ruled that he had told the truth and therefore was not guilty of fostering an ill opinion of the government.

9. Benjamin Franklin epitomized the Enlightenment.

10. Locke argued that people were born neither good nor evil but were shaped toward one or the other by their environment.

Essay Questions

1. What factors contributed to the growth of the colonial population in the seventeenth century?

2. Compare and contrast the status of women, indentured servants, and slaves.

3. Explain the Puritans' major beliefs and describe how they affected life in New England.

4. Compare and contrast colonial agriculture in the southern, middle, and New England colonies.

5. Why were towns and cities important in colonial America?

6. Did the Great Awakening or the Enlightenment have the greater impact on the colonies? Be sure to justify your answer.

ANSWERS TO MULTIPLE-CHOICE AND TRUE-FALSE QUESTIONS

Multiple-Choice Questions

1-A, 2-C, 3-B, 4-D, 5-B, 6-C, 7-B, 8-A, 9-B, 10-C

True-False Questions

1-F, 2-F, 3-F, 4-T, 5-T, 6-F, 7-F, 8-T, 9-T, 10-T

4 ∾

THE IMPERIAL PERSPECTIVE

CHAPTER OBJECTIVES

After you finish reading and studying this chapter, you should be able to

1. Understand the extent and limits of British political and economic control of the colonies.

2. Delineate the major institutions of colonial government in the mother country.

3. Explain the major institutions of colonial government in the colonies.

4. Assess the general relations between the British settlers and the Indians.

5. Describe the nature of French colonization of North America and compare France's colonial policy with Britain's.

6. Discuss the general course of the conflict for empire between France and Britain, and indicate why the British won.

7. Analyze the consequences of Britain's victory in its Great War for Empire with France.

CHAPTER OUTLINE

I. English administration of the colonies
   A. British government
      1. Role of the king
      2. Inconsistent policies
   B. Colonial economic policy
      1. Assumptions of the mercantile system

      2. Provisions of the Navigation Acts of 1651, 1660, 1663, and 1673
      3. Problems with enforcement of the acts
  C. The Dominion of New England
      1. Plans for the Dominion
      2. Errors of Governor Andros
  D. Impact of the Glorious Revolution
      1. Effects on the Dominion of New England
      2. Long-term effects on American history
      3. John Locke's theory
  E. Emergence of a coherent colonial system
      1. Provisions of the Navigation Act of 1696
      2. Role of the Board of Trade
      3. Decline of the policy of "salutary neglect"

II. Colonial self-government
  A. General organization of colonial governments
  B. Powers of the governors
      1. Veto power
      2. Relating to meetings of the assembly
      3. Appointment of council
      4. Judicial powers
      5. Executive powers
  C. Role of the assembly
      1. Method of election
      2. Control of taxes and expenditures
      3. Development of self-government as a "right"

III. Relations with the Indians, the Spanish, and the French
  A. Nature of contacts with the Indians
  B. Major battles with Indians
      1. Early Virginia and Connecticut conflicts
      2. King Philip's War in New England
      3. Bacon's Rebellion, a civil war and an Indian war
  C. Failure of Spain in North America
      1. Emphasis in missions, forts, and gold
      2. Lack of settlements and market economy
  D. Competing with the French
      1. Nature of French settlements in the New World
      2. Control of the Great Lakes and the Mississippi River
      3. Comparison of French and British advantages

IV. Colonial Wars
  A. Four European and intercolonial wars, 1689–1763
      1. Causes
      2. Effects of the conflicts

B. The final war: French and Indian War, 1754–1763
   1. Outbreak of the war
   2. Importance of the Albany Congress
   3. Acadians (Cajuns) exiled by conflict in Canada
   4. Nature of the war in Europe
   5. Role of British sea power
   6. Battle of Quebec and other British victories
   7. The Peace of Paris and results of the war

KEY ITEMS OF CHRONOLOGY

Bacon's Rebellion	1675–1676
Glorious Revolution	1689
King William's War	1689–1697
John Locke, *Two Treatises on Government*	1690
Board of Trade established	1696
Queen Anne's War	1702–1713
King George's War	1744–1748
French and Indian War	1754–1763
Washington surrendered Fort Necessity	1754
Albany Congress	1754
Peace of Paris	1763

TERMS TO MASTER

Listed below are some important people or terms with which you should be familiar after your study of the chapter. Identify each name or term.

1. mercantilism
2. Navigation Acts
3. Lords of Trade
4. Dominion of New England
5. Sir Edmund Andros
6. Glorious Revolution
7. William and Mary
8. John Locke
9. contract theory of government
10. writs of assistance
11. Board of Trade
12. Hanoverian monarchs
13. Robert Walpole
14. "salutary neglect"
15. Bacon's Rebellion
16. William Berkeley
17. acadians
18. Queen Anne's War
19. King George's War
20. French and Indian War
21. Fort Necessity
22. Albany Congress
23. Peace of Paris

VOCABULARY BUILDING

Listed below are some words or phrases used in this chapter. Look in the dictionary for the meaning of each term you do not know.

1. derive
2. fester
3. rationale
4. prerogative
5. revert
6. anomaly
7. prorogue
8. tyranny
9. encroach
10. ravage

11. crony
12. genocidal
13. lucrative
14. savor
15. impede
16. carnage
17. jingoistic
18. incursion
19. athwart
20. bulwark

EXERCISES FOR UNDERSTANDING

When you have finished reading the chapter, answer each of the following questions. If you have difficulty, go back to the text and reread the section of the chapter related to the question.

Multiple-Choice Questions

Select the letter of the response that best completes the statement.

1. Under the Navigation Acts, cotton, indigo, and sugar
   A. could only be produced in the West Indies.
   B. could only be exported to England or its colonies.
   C. could not be produced in the American colonies.
   D. were heavily taxed as imports into the colonies.

2. Legal authority over the American colonies rested with
   A. the British Parliament.
   B. the king of England.
   C. the colonial assemblies.
   D. the Privy Council.

3. Mercantilism involves all of the following *except*
   A. a mother country developing and protecting its own shipping.
   B. a belief that the world's wealth equals the amount of gold and silver available.
   C. an expectation that colonies will supply raw materials to the mother country.
   D. a mother country developing only those products it can produce cheaply and efficiently.

4. The Dominion of New England came to an end with
   A. the death of Charles II.
   B. Bacon's Rebellion.
   C. the Glorious Revolution.
   D. the passage of the Navigation Acts.

5. John Locke's theories
   A. appealed to colonial Americans.
   B. viewed government as a guardian of people's natural rights.
   C. justified overthrowing a government under certain conditions.
   D. all of the above

6. Except for race and gender, the chief restriction on voting in the colonies was
   A. ownership of property.
   B. religious faith.
   C. literacy.
   D. personal friendship.

7. Bacon's Rebellion in Virginia was an example of
   A. the frontier region against the Tidewater area.
   B. common men versus aristocrats.
   C. political outsiders fighting entrenched power.
   D. all the above

8. The Spanish colonial empire in North America declined because Spain
   A. paid too little attention to military affairs.
   B. adhered to a mercantilist policy.
   C. was distracted by huge gold discoveries.
   D. sent too many settlers to its colonies.

9. French colonial policy in North America primarily focused on
   A. rapidly settling the area around the Great Lakes with people loyal to France.
   B. developing fur trading and missionary work rather than colonization.
   C. making treaties with the Indians to gain rights to their lands for future French settlements.
   D. establishing a route westward across the entire North American continent.

10. In the colonial wars, the area that suffered the most was
    A. the backcountry.
    B. the Chesapeake.
    C. New England.
    D. the South.

True-False Questions

Indicate whether each of the following statements is true or false.

1. England hoped to use the Navigation Acts to enforce mercantilism.

2. John Locke devised the contract theory of government.

3. The Glorious Revolution had no significant effect in America.

4. Although the king never vetoed acts of Parliament after 1707, the royal governors still had the power of veto over the colonial legislatures.

5. Disagreements over mercantilism led to King Philip's War.

6. A smaller proportion of the population could vote in the colonies than in England.

7. The French developed better relationships with Indians than did the English.

8. At the Albany Congress, George Washington revealed the colonists' strategy in the French and Indian War.

9. The French and Indian War eliminated the French as a threat to the colonies from the west.

10. The Peace of Paris ended Spanish power in North America.

Essay Questions

1. What was mercantilism? How did it affect the American colonies?

2. How much self-government did the colonists have and what caused it to increase or decrease from the 1650s to the 1750s?

3. How did France's colonial policies differ from the British policies?

4. How did British imperial policy change from 1651 to 1763? What important factors prompted each of the changes?

5. What were the issues in the four major colonial wars, and how did the wars affect the colonies?

ANSWERS TO MULTIPLE-CHOICE
AND TRUE-FALSE QUESTIONS

Multiple-Choice Questions

1-B, 2-B, 3-D, 4-C, 5-D, 6-A, 7-D, 8-B, 9-A, 10-C

True-False Questions

1-T, 2-T, 3-F, 4-T, 5-F, 6-F, 7-T, 8-F, 9-T, 10-F

5

FROM EMPIRE TO INDEPENDENCE

CHAPTER OBJECTIVES

After you finish reading and studying this chapter, you should be able to

1. Explain how the British victory over France in the Great War for Empire, the new government of George III, and other factors worked together to produce Grenville's program.

2. Account for and assess the importance of colonial reaction to the Grenville program, and especially the stamp tax.

3. Analyze the counterplay of British actions and colonial reactions from the repeal of the stamp tax to the Revolution in 1775.

4. Assess British and colonial responsibility for the coming of the Revolution.

CHAPTER OUTLINE

I. Impact of the Great War for Empire
   A. Attitudes of colonists
      1. Self-importance
      2. Separate identity
   B. Problems of British
      1. Governing new lands
      2. Political instability
      3. Indians
   C. Proclamation of 1763
   D. Retaliation of the British government for colonial actions during the war

       1. Imperial forces won the war while colonists traded with the enemy

       2. Efforts to use writs of assistance to stop illegal trade

    E. Colonists used the war to exact concessions from their governors

    F. Problems of managing defense in the newly captured lands to the north and east

II. Grenville's program

    A. Paying for American defense

       1. Making customs collection efficient

       2. The Sugar Act of 1764

       3. The Currency Act of 1764

       4. The Stamp Act of 1765

       5. The Quartering Act of 1765

    B. Colonial reaction

       1. Radical ideals of the "Real Whigs"

       2. Colonial perceptions of the Grenville program

       3. Basis for the argument "no taxation without representation"

    C. The Stamp Act Crisis

       1. Early mass actions

       2. Efforts to unify the protests, the Stamp Act Congress

       3. Use of nonimportation

       4. Repeal of the Stamp Act

       5. Meaning of the Declaratory Act

III. The Townshend Acts

    A. Changing politics in England

    B. Basis for and provisions of the Townshend Acts, 1767

    C. Colonial reactions

       1. Dickinson's *Letters* oppose taxes for revenue

       2. Samuel Adams and the Sons of Liberty

       3. Virginia Resolves

       4. Boston Massacre, 1770

       5. Repeal of the Townshend Duties except on tea, 1770

       6. Improved relations, tinder awaiting a spark

IV. Backcountry discontent

    A. Ethan Allen and the creation of Vermont, 1777

    B. Paxton Boys' rebellion in Pennsylvania

    C. Evidences of discontent in the Carolinas

V. Renewed tension with England

    A. Burning of the *Gaspee*

    B. Formation of the Committees of correspondence

    C. Lord North and the Tea Act of 1773

       1. Terms of the act

       2. Nature of colonial reactions

      3. Boston Tea Party, 1773
  D. The Coercive Acts, 1774
  E. Quebec Act prevents entry to western lands
  F. Colonial actions of support for Boston
  G. The First Continental Congress, September 1774
      1. All colonies represented except Georgia
      2. Endorse Suffolk Resolves
      3. Adopt Continental Association
      4. Call a second Congress for May 1775
      5. British reactions

VI. Colonists take the initiative
  A. Strengthening colonial militias
  B. Battles of Lexington and Concord
  C. Capture of Fort Ticonderoga
  D. Actions of the Second Continental Congress
  E. Battle of Bunker Hill
  F. Congress's two documents of explanation
  G. British army retreated
  H. Impact of Thomas Paine's *Common Sense*
  I. The Declaration of Independence
      1. Jefferson's draft
      2. Modifications
      3. Contract theory of government

VII. Assessment of the causes of the Revolution

KEY ITEMS OF CHRONOLOGY

Proclamation Line to close settlement beyond the mountains	1763
Sugar Act	1764
Stamp Act and Stamp Act Congress	1765
Virginia Resolves	1765
Repeal of Stamp Act and passage of Declaratory Act	1766
Townshend Acts	1767
John Dickinson's *Letters of a Pennsylvania Farmer*	1767
Boston Massacre	March 1770
Repeal of Townshend duties by Lord North	April 1770
Gaspee incident	1772
Tea Act (of Lord North)	1773
Boston Tea Party	1773
Coercive Acts (Intolerable Acts)	1774
First Continental Congress	September 1774

Military confrontation at Lexington	April 19, 1775
Second Continental Congress	May 1775
Battle of Bunker Hill	June 1775
Publication of Thomas Paine's *Common Sense*	January 1776
Declaration of Independence adopted	July 2, 1776

TERMS TO MASTER

Listed below are some important people or terms with which you should be familiar after your study of the chapter. Identify each name or term.

1. George Grenville
2. Sugar Act
3. Stamp Act
4. Virginia Resolves
5. Stamp Act Congress
6. Whig ideology
7. virtual representation
8. external and internal taxes
9. William Pitt (Earl of Chatham)
10. Townshend Acts
11. *Letters of a Pennsylvania Farmer*
12. Samuel Adams
13. Sons of Liberty
14. Boston Massacre
15. Crispus Attucks
16. Paxton Boys
17. Regulators
18. *Gaspee*
19. Boston Tea Party
20. Committees of Correspondence
21. Coercive Acts
22. Continental Congress
23. Tories
24. Continental Association
25. Lexington and Concord
26. Battle of Bunker Hill
27. Olive Branch Petition
28. *Common Sense*
29. Thomas Paine
30. Delaration of Independence
31. Hessians

VOCABULARY BUILDING

Listed below are some words or phrases used in this chapter. Look in the dictionary for the meaning of each term you do not know.

1. euphoria
2. pacify
3. currency
4. rampant
5. salutary
6. alleviate
7. deflationary
8. unwittingly
9. effigy
10. leverage
11. frugality
12. stevedore
13. indefatigable
14. indict
15. tinder
16. vigilante
17. disputatious
18. wanton
19. gauntlet
20. discretion

EXERCISES FOR UNDERSTANDING

When you have finished reading the chapter, answer each of the following questions. If you have difficulty, go back to the text and reread the section of the chapter related to the question.

Multiple-Choice Questions

Select the letter of the response that best completes the statement.

1. In the aftermath of the Great War for Empire, the British
   A. could depend on the loyalty of the colonists.
   B. had the benefit of great statesmanship under George III.
   C. faced problems dealing with the new western lands.
   D. enjoyed a budget surplus from trade with the western lands.

2. The Proclamation of 1763
   A. barred settlement west of the Appalachians.
   B prohibited colonies from issuing their own money.
   C. prompted the formation of the Sons of Liberty.
   D. required colonists to supply British troops in America.

3. The Stamp Act most directly affected
   A. farmers, who would need stamps to take produce to market.
   B. lawyers and other articulate groups, who could arouse the population.
   C. officeholders under the English government, who would need the stamps to carry on their work.
   D. smugglers, who could not continue their activities without buying the stamps.

4. The colonists' argument against the Townshend duties was
   A. that the British government could impose taxes on the colonies only to regulate trade, not to raise revenue.
   B. that there should never be a tax on tea because it was a patriotic drink.
   C. presented primarily by Thomas Paine.
   D. that the British had no right to use taxes to regulate trade in the colonies.

5. In response to the Townshend Acts, John Dickinson's *Letters of a Pennsylvania Farmer* sought to
   A. spur colonists on the frontier to protest, even to revolt against the British.
   B. organize the Sons of Liberty.
   C. propose a moderate resolution to the colonial disagreements.
   D. rally support for the British imperial authority.

6. According to the royal governor, "the most dangerous man in Massachusetts" in the late 1760s was
   A. Thomas Paine.
   B. Samuel Adams.
   C. Crispus Attucks.
   D. Paul Revere.

7. The aggressive violence of the Green Mountain Boys, the Paxton Boys, and the Regulators
   A. demonstrated divisions among the colonists.
   B. scared and intimidated the British authorities in the colonies.
   C. proved colonial unity.
   D. none of the above

8. The First Continental Congress meeting in Philadelphia in September 1774
   A. used voting on the basis of population rather than one vote for each colony.
   B. asserted that Parliament had a right to impose internal taxes and regulations on the colonies so long as they were only to raise revenue.
   C. urged creation of a Continental Association in all colonies to enforce the boycott of British goods.
   D. declared the United States to be free and independent of Britain.

9. One effect of the Battle of Bunker Hill in 1775 was to
   A. make English generals more aggressive.
   B. divide colonists between Loyalists and Patriots.
   C. prompt the formation of the First Continental Congress.
   D. all of the above

10. In the Declaration of Independence, Thomas Jefferson drew heavily on the ideas of
    A. Thomas Paine.
    B. George Grenville and Horace Walpole.
    C. John Dickinson.
    D. John Locke.

True-False Questions

Indicate whether each statement is true or false.

1. One effect of the Great War for Empire was that the colonists felt greater allegiance to the British empire.

2. George Grenville followed a policy of salutary neglect.

3. For the first time, the Sugar Act of 1764 deliberately sought to raise revenue in the colonies, not just regulate colonial trade.

4. In repealing the Stamp Act, Parliament forfeited all power to make laws affecting the colonies.

5. The colonial "Real Whigs" believed the British army was tyrannical.

6. Backcountry dissent in the colonies was primarily aimed at the lack of services that the coastal areas were providing for people living on the frontier.

7. The Boston Tea Party occurred before the Boston Massacre.

8. Hessians were German soldiers who fought in support of the colonists.

9. The war for American independence started after the Continental Congress adopted the Declaration of Independence.

10. One important factor leading to the adoption of the Declaration of Independence was the realization by the Americans that they needed to be independent in order to trade with France and other countries.

Essay Questions

1. How did British colonial policies fail and consequently help cause the American Revolution?

2. Explain the developing arguments American colonists used against British colonial policies between the Great War for Empire and the American Revolution.

3. Trace the major stages in the growing sense of colonial unity against the British from 1760 to 1776.

4. What explanations have historians offered for the causes of the American Revolution? Which make the most sense?

5. In your own words, write a concise summary of the argument for independence developed in the Declaration of Independence. Be sure to read the explanation in the text of the reasoning used in the Declaration. Then read the document itself in the text's Appendix.

ANSWERS TO MULTIPLE-CHOICE
AND TRUE-FALSE QUESTIONS

Multiple-Choice Questions

1-C, 2-A, 3-B, 4-A, 5-C, 6-B, 7-A, 8-C, 9-B, 10-D

True-False Questions

1-F, 2-F, 3-T, 4-F, 5-T, 6-F, 7-F, 8-F, 9-F, 10-T

THE AMERICAN REVOLUTION

CHAPTER OBJECTIVES

After you finish reading and studying this chapter, you should be able to

1. Explain the major military strategies of the war, especially focusing on the turning points.

2. Account for the division of sentiments in the colonial population during the war.

3. Assess the degree to which the Revolution was a social revolution—the impact of the war on slavery, women, religion, and socioeconomic levels.

4. Identify the governmental principles incorporated into the new national and state governments.

5. Describe America's postwar nationalism and show its impact on various aspects of American culture.

CHAPTER OUTLINE

I. The campaigns of 1776
   A. Comparison of the two armies
   B. Howe's force in New York
   C. Washington's minor victories in New Jersey

II. Effects of the war on society
   A. Size and nature of the Loyalist population
   B. Internal conflicts between groups of colonists
   C. Nature of the militias and the Continental Army
   D. Methods of financing the war

E. Ways of surviving the winter of 1776–77
F. Impact of the war on different social groups
1. Sacrifices required
2. Opportunities for profit
3. Social equality versus inequality

III. Expansion of the war in 1777
A. The British plan of attack
B. Howe in Philadelphia
C. Washington at Valley Forge
D. American victory at Saratoga
E. Southern campaign
F. France enters the war
1. Importance of Saratoga victory
2. Details of the treaty with France
3. Spain joins France on the American side

IV. The stalemate of 1778
A. Winter at Valley Forge
B. Changes in British policy
1. Peace Commission to the Americans
2. Evacuation of Philadelphia as Clinton replaces Howe
C. The war in the West
1. Victories of George Rogers Clark
2. Destruction of the Iroquois
3. Daniel Boone in Kentucky

V. The war turns south
A. British move south
B. Fighting in the Carolinas
1. British take Charleston
2. Gates defeated at Camden
3. Forces of Cornwallis and Greene fight
C. Benedict Arnold's treachery
D. The victory of Yorktown, October 1781

VI. The road to a peace settlement
A. Negotiators
B. Complications in the negotiations
C. Terms of the Peace of Paris, September 3, 1783

VII. The political revolution
A. Republican ideology
1. Debate over form of government
2. Balanced polity and civic virtue

B. State constitutions
  1. Experimentation
  2. Separation of powers
  3. Bills of rights
C. Adoption of the Articles of Confederation

VIII. The extent of the social revolution
  A. Differing expectations of the Revolution
  B. Extension of equality to lower groups
    1. Expanded suffrage
    2. Disposal of land tracts
  C. Impact on slavery
    1. Importation of slaves ended in all states but Georgia
    2. Role of blacks in the war
    3. Antislavery sentiment
  D. Impact on women
    1. Limitations on women in the eighteenth century
    2. Role of women in the war
    3. Limited legal gains made for women
  E. Impact on religion
    1. Separation of the Anglican church from the state governments
    2. Growth of national church organizations

IX. Sense of nationalism inspired by the Revolution
  A. Independence Day
  B. Growth of education, a more lasting effect
    1. Development of state universities
    2. Impetus for state-supported lower schools
  C. The new mission of America

KEY ITEMS OF CHRONOLOGY

Congress adopted Declaration of Independence	July 2, 1776
Thomas Paine's *The American Crisis*	1776
Battle of Saratoga	October 1777
Winter at Valley Forge	1777–1778
Alliance with France	February 1778
Battle of Monmouth County Courthouse	June 1778
Battle of King's Mountain	October 1780
Articles of Confederation adopted	March 1781
Battle of Yorktown	October 1781
Peace of Paris	1783

TERMS TO MASTER

Listed below are some important people or terms with which you should be familiar after your study of the chapter. Identify each name or term.

1. *The American Crisis*
2. Hessians
3. Loyalists
4. Whigs
5. militia
6. Continental Army
7. Battle of Saratoga
8. Henry Clinton
9. George Rogers Clark
10. Horatio Gates
11. Lord Cornwallis
12. Battle of King's Mountain
13. sovereignty
14. John Paul Jones
15. Battle of Yorktown
16. Peace of Paris
17. republican ideology
18. Articles of Confederation
19. Constitutional Convention
20. Noah Webster

VOCABULARY BUILDING

Listed below are some words or phrases used in this chapter. Look in the dictionary for the meaning of each term you do not know.

1. formidable
2. insurgent
3. fratricidal
4. marauding
5. augment
6. fervor
7. conscript
8. aggrandizement
9. insatiable
10. austerity
11. odious
12. veneration
13. amity
14. bivouac
15. latent
16. attrition
17. scruples
18. spawn
19. manumit
20. pluralistic

EXERCISES FOR UNDERSTANDING

When you have finished reading the chapter, answer each of the following questions. If you have difficulty, go back to the text and reread the section of the chapter related to the question.

Multiple-Choice Questions

Select the letter of the choice that best completes the statement.

1. At the outset of the Revolution, Washington and his army escaped New York because of
   A. General Washington's astute strategy.
   B. British general Howe's caution.
   C. the intervention of the French.
   D. the good fortune of a harsh winter.

2. "These are the times that try men's souls," declared
   A. George Washington at Valley Forge.
   B. Thomas Paine in *The American Crisis.*
   C. Benedict Arnold after the Battle of Saratoga.
   D. the Declaration of Independence.

3. During the war,
   A. there was little temptation to speculate or make fortunes off the situation.
   B. there was a strong desire on the part of colonial leaders to have social equality and end distinctions of birth and wealth.
   C. the militias remained the best organized and disciplined military groups on the colonial side.
   D. because of deserters and limited enlistments, Washington's army fluctuated in size from 5,000 to 20,000.

4. The battle of Saratoga was a turning point in the war because it
   A. encouraged the French to help the colonists.
   B. demonstrated American naval superiority.
   C. brought the Indians into the war on the Patriots' side.
   D. all of the above

5. In 1782 negotiations to end the war were complicated by
   A. American military setbacks.
   B. Jefferson's dominance of diplomatic maneuvers in Europe.
   C. relations between Spain and France.
   D. the House of Commons's insistence on continuing the war.

6. The American Revolution was
   A. fought only between the British and the Americans.
   B. a war primarily among the colonists.
   C. a world war.
   D. not really a war but a series of small skirmishes.

7. The Articles of Confederation
   A. placed great power in the national congress.
   B. failed to establish a system of courts.
   C. created a weak president.
   D. severely restricted the power of the individual states.

8. One result of the Revolution was
   A. a general extension of the right to vote to women.
   B. an expansion of the importation of slaves.
   C. a strengthening of patterns of deference.
   D. a widespread emancipation of northern slaves.

9. New state governments created during the Revolution
   A. gave increased power to the executives.
   B. created governments based on written constitutions.
   C. were committed to providing substantial funds to the national government.
   D. generally provided full equality for women and landless men.

10. In American religion, the Revolution contributed to
    A. greater separation of church and state.
    B. the creation of national church organizations.
    C. complete freedom of religion.
    D. all of the above

True-False Questions

Indicate whether each statement is true or false.

1. In the Revolution, the Americans lost most of the battles but won the war.

2. Most American Tories left the colonies during the Revolution.

3. In the American Revolution, Whigs and Loyalists were the same.

4. General "Gentleman Johnny" Burgoyne led American forces at Saratoga.

5. The greatest American loss in the war was at Charleston.

6. Slaves were not permitted to serve in the American armed forces during the Revolution.

7. The northern colonies were more valuable to the British Empire because they produced staple crops.

8. As a result of the Revolution, the Americans instituted universal manhood suffrage.

9. Women provided many examples of individual heroism during the Revolutionary War, but their overall legal status did not improve greatly from the war.

10. During the Revolution all state support for religion ended.

Essay Questions

1. Identify several key events or turning points in the Revolutionary War and explain their importance to the outcome of the war.

2. Which was more important, the war in the colonies north of Philadelphia or the fighting in the southern colonies?

3. What was the republican ideology that developed in the Revolutionary era and how did it affect political developments after independence?

4. In what ways was the Revolution a world war? Did the international aspects of the Revolution affect its outcome?

5. How did the War for Independence effect changes in American society? Assess its importance as a social revolution.

ANSWERS TO MULTIPLE-CHOICE AND TRUE-FALSE QUESTIONS

Multiple-Choice Questions

1-B, 2-B, 3-D, 4-A, 5-C, 6-C, 7-B, 8-D, 9-B, 10-D

True-False Questions

1-T, 2-F, 3-F, 4-F, 5-T, 6-F, 7-F, 8-F, 9-F, 10-T

7

SHAPING A FEDERAL UNION

CHAPTER OBJECTIVES

After you finish reading and studying this chapter, you should be able to

1. Analyze the strengths and weaknesses of the government under the Articles of Confederation.

2. Describe the key accomplishments of the Confederation government in diplomacy, governmental organization, land policy, and finance.

3. List and explain the major problems that the Confederation government faced in finance and diplomacy.

4. Account for the movement to adopt a new constitution and assess the degree to which a new government was needed.

5. Analyze the principles considered and incorporated in the Constitution.

6. Account for the success of the movement to ratify the Constitution.

CHAPTER OUTLINE

I. Government under the Articles of Confederation
   A. The role of Congress
      1. Strengths and weaknesses
      2. Accomplishments
      3. Development of a committee system
      4. Organization of three departments
   B. Finance in the Confederation government
      1. Role of Robert Morris, superintendent of finance
      2. Reasons for failure to get financial stability

   3. Growth of the congressional debt
C. Development of a land policy
   1. Basis for congressional action
   2. Provisions of three major ordinances
      a. Land surveying and sales
      b. System of territorial government
   3. A system for lands south of the Ohio River
   4. Obtaining claims to Indian lands
D. Economic life under the Confederation
   1. The war's impact on agriculture
   2. Problems of merchants
   3. Trade with Britain and others
   4. Development of small-scale American manufacturing
E. Diplomacy under the Articles
   1. British irritants
   2. Conflicts with Spain
F. Other problems
   1. Need to promote domestic manufactures
   2. Demands for currency or other legal tender
   3. Causes and importance of Shays's Rebellion
G. Calls for a change in government
   1. Advocacy of strong government
   2. Federalists or nationalists
   3. Preliminary meetings
   4. Call for a convention

II. Drafting the Constitution
A. Characteristics of the convention
   1. Delegates and their organization
   2. Political philosophies
   3. Organization of the convention
   4. Decision for secrecy
   5. Madison's role
B. Conflicts among major plans
   1. Provisions of the Virginia Plan
   2. Provisions of the New Jersey Plan
   3. Content of the Connecticut Compromise
C. The conflict over slavery leads to the three-fifths compromise
D. Lack of consideration given to women
E. Features of the new government
   1. Separation of powers
   2. Nature of the bicameral Congress
   3. Role of the executive
   4. Provisions for the judiciary

5. Concept of countervailing forces
6. Basis for ratification
F. The fight for ratification
   1. Characteristics of Federalists and Antifederalists
   2. Motivation of the framers
   3. Arguments of *The Federalist*
   4. The process of ratification
   5. The genius of the Constitution

KEY ITEMS OF CHRONOLOGY

Adam Smith's *The Wealth of Nations*	1776
Ratification of the Articles of Confederation	1781
Peace with Britain (formal end to Revolution)	1783
Land Ordinance of 1785	1785
Northwest Ordinance	1787
Shays's Rebellion	January 1787
Constitutional Convention 1787	May–September
The Federalist	1787–1788
Ninth state (New Hampshire) ratified the Constitution	June 1788
Virginia and New York ratified the Constitution	June–July 1788
New government set to commence	March 1789

TERMS TO MASTER

Listed below are some important people or terms with which you should be familiar after your study of the chapter. Identify each name or term.

1. Critical Period
2. Articles of Confederation
3. Robert Morris
4. Land Ordinance of 1785
5. Northwest Ordinance
6. *The Wealth of Nations*
7. Shays's Rebellion
8. Constitutional Convention
9. James Wilson
10. checks and balances
11. Virginia and New Jersey Plans
12. the Great Compromise
13. Nationalists (Federalists) and Antifederalists
14. separation of powers
15. Charles A. Beard
16. James Madison
17. Alexander Hamilton
18. *The Federalist*, No. 10

VOCABULARY BUILDING

Listed below are some words or phrases used in this chapter. Look in the dictionary for the meaning of each term you do not know.

1. quorum
2. privateering
3. levy
4. cession
5. clamor
6. tutelage
7. rescind
8. disgruntled
9. pillage
10. ingrain
11. aggregate
12. magisterial
13. swelter
14. bind
15. contentious
16. apportion
17. disdain
18. staggered (adj.)
19. indict
20. countervailing

EXERCISES FOR UNDERSTANDING

When you have finished reading the chapter, answer each of the following questions. If you have difficulty, go back to the text and reread the section of the chapter related to the question.

Multiple-Choice Questions

Select the letter of the response that best completes the statement.

1. The Articles of Confederation established a government that
   A. gave too much power to the national Congress.
   B. was a total failure.
   C. had power in the United States from 1781 to 1787.
   D. all of the above

2. The Northwest Ordinance was significant in part because it
   A. gave free land to former slaves.
   B. barred disloyal Tories from the western territories.
   C. set a procedure for territories to become states.
   D. established a precedent for protecting the rights of Native Americans.

3. The classic attack on mercantilism came in
   A. *The Federalist.*
   B. the Annapolis Convention.
   C. the New Jersey Plan.
   D. *The Wealth of Nations.*

4. Shays's Rebellion in Massachusetts
   A. represented a revolt against the lax government of the Articles of Confederation.
   B. was largely triggered by a currency shortage among farmers.
   C. led to the governor's being captured and held for five days.
   D. is correctly represented by *all* of the above.

5. "The tree of liberty must be refreshed from time to time with the blood of patriots and tyrants," said
   A. John Adams.
   B. Alexander Hamilton.
   C. Thomas Jefferson.
   D. George Washington.

6. By the middle 1780s, Federalists came to realize that the government
   A. had to be based on the virtue of a few citizens instead of the many.
   B. under the Articles of Confederation had succeeded.
   C. had to avoid tyrannical central authority.
   D. all of the above

7. Except for George Washington, perhaps the most influential delegate to the Constitutional Convention was
   A. Thomas Jefferson.
   B. Alexander Hamilton.
   C. Benjamin Franklin.
   D. James Wilson.

8. The first and most important issue the Constitutional Convention had to decide was
   A. whether to allow slavery to continue in the United States.
   B. how representation should be apportioned.
   C. whether to count slaves as people for purposes of representation.
   D. the status of Indians in the new nation.

9. The Constitutional Convention dealt with slavery by agreeing to
   A. abolish slavery in the southern states.
   B. count each slave as three-fifths of a person in apportioning taxes and representatives.
   C. ignore the issue entirely.
   D. allow slavery in the territories but not in the original thirteen states.

10. Patrick Henry, Samuel Adams, and Elbridge Gerry
    A. supported the new Constitution.
    B. stressed the weaknesses of the Articles of Confederation.
    C. contributed to *The Federalist.*
    D. were Antifederalists.

True-False Questions

Indicate whether each statement is true or false.

1. The Congress of the Confederation always operated at a budget deficit.

2. After the Revolutionary War the Americans happily found themselves able to trade with Britain and its colonies on the same terms as when they were colonists.

3. After the Revolution, problems with Spain included navigation of the Mississippi River.

4. Probably the greatest economic needs during the Confederation period were for greater amounts of currency in circulation and more opportunity for people to obtain credit.

5. Mechanics and merchants wanted a stronger central government to provide uniform trade regulations.

6. At the Constitutional Convention, the Virginia Plan called for a two-house Congress with considerable powers.

7. The Great Compromise at the Constitutional Convention involved representation in the House and the Senate.

8. Leading nationalists included James Madison, James Wilson, and Alexander Hamilton.

9. In *The Federalist* No. 1, Madison argued that the nation's size would insure no single faction could dominate the government.

10. *The Federalist* supported the Articles of Confederation and opposed the new Constitution.

Essay Questions

1. Evaluate the weaknesses of the government under the Articles of Confederation and explain the effects of the Critical Period on the creation of the Constitution.

2. What were the accomplishments of the government under the Articles of Confederation?

3. Explain the major compromises of the Constitutional Convention.

4. How do the three branches of government (legislative, executive, and judicial) serve as checks and balances on each other?

5. Explain the significance of the major principles of government incorporated into the Constitution.

6. What was the procedure followed to ratify the Constitution? Why did the people decide ratification was necessary?

ANSWERS TO MULTIPLE-CHOICE AND TRUE-FALSE QUESTIONS

Multiple-Choice Questions

1-C, 2-C, 3-D, 4-B, 5-C, 6-A, 7-D, 8-B, 9-B, 10-D

True-False Questions

1-T, 2-F, 3-T, 4-F, 5-T, 6-T, 7-T, 8-T, 9-T, 10-F

8

THE FEDERALIST ERA

CHAPTER OBJECTIVES

After you finish reading and studying this chapter, you should be able to

1. Explain the challenge that confronted the Washington administration in creating a new government.

2. Name and summarize the three major proposals presented by Alexander Hamilton for establishing the new government on a sound financial basis.

3. Analyze the conflict of philosophy between Hamilton and Jefferson over the constitutionality of the national bank and explain how that conflict led to the development of two political parties.

4. Account for the diplomatic problems with Britain, France, and Spain that buffeted the new nation, and explain the resolution of each.

5. Assess the differing roles played by Adams, Hamilton, and Washington in Federalist politics and describe their effects on Adams's administration.

6. Understand the significance of the elections of 1796 and 1800.

7. Explain the importance of the Alien and Sedition Acts and the Kentucky and Virginia Resolutions as parts of continuing conflicts between individual liberty and governmental authority, and states' rights versus national governmental authority.

CHAPTER OUTLINE

I. The new United States
   A. Regional differences

    B. Demographics
       1. Rural
       2. African Americans
       3. Indians
       4. The West
    C. The new government
       1. Washington and his governing style
       2. Status of the bureaucracy in 1789
       3. Makeup of Washington's cabinet
       4. Congress approves the Bill of Rights
          a. Response to Antifederalists
          b. George Mason
          c. Protection of individual rights

II. Hamilton's vision of America
    A. Personal background
    B. Report on the Public Credit, 1790
       1. His plan to fund the national debt and assume the state debts
       2. Justifications for Hamilton's debt plan
       3. Reactions to Hamilton's plan
       4. Nature of the compromise approved
    C. Hamilton's plan for a national bank
       1. Nature of Hamilton's plan
       2. Reactions in Congress
       3. Jefferson's and Hamilton's arguments regarding constitutionality of
          the proposal
       4. Disposition of the proposal
    D. Hamilton's Report on Manufactures
       1. Rationale for the program
       2. Means of stimulating manufactures
       3. Arguments about his scheme
       4. Disposition of the proposal
    E. Assessing Hamilton's achievements

III. Development of political parties
    A. Attitudes toward parties
    B. Emergence of rivalry: Hamilton v. Madison and Jefferson
    C. Jefferson's background and outlook
    D. Jefferson and Hamilton compared

IV. Crises foreign and domestic
    A. Foreign affairs
       1. The French Revolution
          a. Outbreak of hostilities between France and Britain
          b. American neutrality

      c. Nature of Citizen Genêt Affair

      d. Stance of Republicans and Federalists on foreign affairs

    2. Jay's treaty with Britain

      a. Jay's instructions

      b. Terms accepted by Jay

      c. Reactions to the treaty

  B. Problems with Indians on the frontier

  C. Whiskey Rebellion

    1. Importance of alcoholic drinks

    2. Basis for the rebellion

    3. Efforts to suppress the rebellion

    4. Significance of the episode

  D. Pinckney's Treaty with Spain

  E. Movement into the West

    1. Issues in conflict

    2. Terms of the treaty

V. Settlement of the West

  A. Land policy

    1. Conflict over principles

    2. Political differences

    3. Policies adopted

  B. Wilderness trail

    1. Daniel Boone

    2. Settlement of Kentucky

VI. Transfer of power

  A. Washington's achievements

  B. Washington's farewell address

  C. Election of 1796

    1. Candidates

    2. Hamilton's scheme

    3. Results

  D. Adams's years

    1. Background and career

    2. Troubles with France

      a. Undeclared war

      b. The XYZ Affair

      c. Stronger military

      d. Peace settlement

    3. Domestic effects of war

      a. Federalists v. Republicans

        i. Emergence of factions

        ii. Personal attacks

b. Alien and Sedition Acts
 i. Terms of laws
 ii. Prosecutions
 iii. Virginia and Kentucky Resolutions
E. Election of 1800
 1. Issues between parties
 2. Candidates
 3. Results
 4. Election of Jefferson and Burr
 5. Packing of judiciary with Federalists
 6. New democratic politics

KEY ITEMS OF CHRONOLOGY

Inauguration of Washington	April 1789
Hamilton's Reports	1790–1791
Ratification of the Bill of Rights	1791
Creation of the Bank of the United States	1791
Citizen Genêt Affair	1793
Jay's Treaty	1794
Whiskey Rebellion	1794
Pinckney's Treaty	1795
Washington's farewell address	1796
John Adams elected	1796
XYZ Affair	1797
Alien and Sedition Acts	1798
Election of Jefferson	1800

TERMS TO MASTER

Listed below are some important people or terms with which you should be familiar after your study of the chapter. Identify each name or term.

1. Thomas Jefferson
2. Alexander Hamilton
3. Bill of Rights
4. Report on a National Bank
5. Report on Manufacturers
6. implied powers
7. Federalists
8. Republicans
9. Citizen Genêt
10. Jay's Treaty
11. Whiskey Rebellion
12. Pinckney's Treaty
13. land policy
14. Wilderness Road
15. Daniel Boone
16. squatters
17. John Adams
18. XYZ Affair

19. Alien and Sedition Acts
20. Kentucky and Virginia Resolutions
21. interposition
22. nullification

VOCABULARY BUILDING

Listed below are some words or phrases used in this chapter. Look in the dictionary for the meaning of each term you do not know.

1. harbor (v.)
2. census
3. homogeneous
4. bureaucracy
5. enumeration
6. disparage
7. stalemate
8. embodiment
9. partisan
10. agronomist
11. primogeniture
12. adjudicate
13. annuity
14. copious
15. smite
16. teem
17. baneful
18. relent
19. credence
20. unscrupulous

EXERCISES FOR UNDERSTANDING

When you have finished reading the chapter, answer each of the following questions. If you have difficulty, go back to the text and reread the section of the chapter related to the question.

Multiple-Choice Questions

Select the letter of the response that best completes the statement.

1. The Bill of Rights was not
   A. advocated by James Madison.
   B. originally written by George Mason.
   C. proposed to satisfy Antifederalists.
   D. designed to protect individual rights.

2. In general, Alexander Hamilton's programs were based on his
   A. own self-interest and the interests of his region.
   B. fondness for farmers and settlers on the frontier.
   C. strong opposition to capitalism and suspicion of monarchy.
   D. nationalist vision and faith in a governing elite.

3. "I am not a friend to a very energetic government," said
   A. George Washington.
   B. Alexander Hamilton.
   C. John Jay.
   D. Thomas Jefferson.

4. In their contest with the Federalists, Republicans generally supported
   A. reason, liberty, and France.
   B. order, religious faith, and Britain.
   C. order, reason, and Britain.
   D. liberty, religious faith, and Britain.

5. The Jay Treaty resolved problems with
   A. Britain over posts in the Northwest.
   B. France over Citizen Genêt's activities in the United States.
   C. Spain over rights on the Mississippi River.
   D. Indians over land rights in the present-day states of Ohio and Indiana.

6. The Whiskey Rebellion was a protest by
   A. backcountry grain farmers in Pennsylvania.
   B. Hamiltonians against Jeffersonian temperance.
   C. importers of rum from the West Indies.
   D. tavern owners against a tax on whiskey.

7. In Congress, James Madison led the
   A. supporters of a strong national government.
   B. critics of Hamilton's policies.
   C. opponents of Jefferson's agrarian vision.
   D. opponents of states' rights.

8. The Alien and Sedition Acts
   A. angered Hamilton and the Federalists.
   B. were ruled unconstitutional by the Supreme Court.
   C. actually affected a small number of people.
   D. helped ensure the reelection of John Adams in 1800.

9. The election of Jefferson in 1800 signaled
   A. a more democratic political system.
   B. an end to partisan differences.
   C. the dominance of the Federalist party.
   D. a return to government controlled by an educated elite.

10. Before the Federalists left office in 1801, they sought to
    A. ratify the Jay Treaty with Great Britain.
    B. declare war on France.
    C. ensure their control of the federal courts.
    D. expand the nation's dominance to the Pacific Ocean.

True-False Questions

Indicate whether each statement is true or false.

1. More than any other crop, cotton experienced the greatest surge in production after 1790.

2. In 1790 almost half of all white Americans were under the age of sixteen.

3. The first great debate over interpreting the Constitution arose over the Alien and Sedition Acts.

4. In the struggle between Hamilton and Jefferson, Washington clearly sided with Jefferson.

5. Hamilton advocated a tax on manufactured exports from the United States.

6. Daniel Boone blazed the Wilderness Road into Kentucky.

7. In his farewell address, Washington urged the United States to steer clear of permanent alliances with European nations, though alliances with Latin America were acceptable.

8. Citizen Genêt made plans to outfit ships against the British navy and schemed with frontiersmen to launch an attack on Spanish Florida.

9. The Jay Treaty of 1794 finally ended the XYZ Affair.

10. The second president was John Adams.

Essay Questions

1. What were the main parts of the new federal government, and what were their main functions?

2. How did Hamilton want the nation to develop? What were his major proposals to achieve his vision for the country?

3. Explain the significance of foreign policy in the first dozen years of the new nation.

4. Why did the first political parties come into existence?

5. Explain the two purposes of United States land policy and show how those purposes created a dilemma. How did the provisions of the land policy change before 1804?

6. How did the Alien and Sedition Acts threaten liberty and how did the Kentucky and Virginia Resolutions defend liberty? Which were correct?

7. How and why did Jefferson and the Republicans win the election in 1800?

ANSWERS TO MULTIPLE-CHOICE
AND TRUE-FALSE QUESTIONS

Multiple-Choice Questions

1-A, 2-D, 3-D, 4-A, 5-A, 6-B, 7-B, 8-C, 9-A, 10-C

True-False Questions

1-T, 2-T, 3-F, 4-T, 5-F, 6-T, 7-F, 8-T, 9-F, 10-T

9 ∽

THE EARLY REPUBLIC

CHAPTER OBJECTIVES

After you finish reading and studying this chapter, you should be able to

1. Assess the impact of Republican control of the government under Jefferson's administration.

2. Understand the growth of the judicial branch under John Marshall and the partisan disputes between Republicans and Federalists over the judiciary.

3. Explain and account for the notable acts of political dissidence in the years 1801–1815.

4. Evaluate the causes of the War of 1812 and draw a conclusion about their relative importance.

5. Explain the impact of the War of 1812 on the United States.

CHAPTER OUTLINE

  I. The dynamic young republic
    A. Westward movement of whites
      1. Land sales
      2. Migrations
        a. From the Old South
        b. Across the Blue Ridge Mountains
        c. From the North
      3. Immobile slaves and servants

      B. Free blacks and Indians

      C. Entrepreneurial spirit

         1. Market economy

         2. End of colonial status

         3. New industries

         4. Commercial nation

  II. Jeffersonian simplicity

      A. The inaugural

         1. Simple ceremony

         2. Inaugural address

      B. The administration

         1. No trappings of monarchy

         2. Still a gentleman

 III. Jefferson in office

      A. The "Revolution of 1800"

         1. Conciliatory policies

         2. Cabinet appointments

         3. Judicial appointments

      B. *Marbury* v. *Madison*

         1. Background to the case

         2. Importance of the ruling

      C. Domestic programs

         1. Acceptance of the national bank

         2. Repeal of excise taxes

         3. Sources of revenue

         4. Reduction of armed forces

         5. Slave trade outlawed

      D. Conflict with the Barbary pirates

      E. The Louisiana Purchase

         1. Negotiations with France

         2. Concern about the constitutional issue

         3. Ratification of the treaty

         4. Forays into Florida

      F. The Lewis and Clark expedition

      G. Federalist political schemes

         1. Concerns of New England

         2. The Essex Junto

         3. The Burr-Hamilton duel, 1804

      H. Reelection of Jefferson, 1804

 IV. Divisions within the Republican party

      A. Basis for Republican dissent

         1. John Randolph

2. The *Tertium Quid*
  B. The Burr Conspiracy
    1. Burr's background and character
    2. Impact of the Hamilton duel
    3. Intrigue with James Wilkinson
    4. Trial for treason
      a. Jefferson's use of "executive privilege"
      b. Rigid definition of treason

V. The war in Europe
  A. Harassment of American shipping by Britain and France
    1. Mutual blockades
    2. Impressment of sailors by Britain
    3. Response to *Chesapeake* incident
  B. Jefferson's embargo, 1807
    1. Public failure to accept
    2. Repeal, March 1, 1809
  C. Election of James Madison
  D. Drift to war
    1. Non-Intercourse Act, 1809
    2. Macon's Bill No. 2, 1810
    3. Intrigues with Britain and France over trade restrictions
  E. Declaration of war, June 1, 1812

VI. War of 1812
  A. Causes
    1. Demand for neutral rights
    2. Sectional support for the war
    3. Indian uprisings and land hunger
    4. Tecumseh loses to Harrison at Tippecanoe
    5. Possible conquest of Canada
    6. National honor
  B. Preparations for war
    1. Financial problems
    2. Poor conditions of the army
    3. State of the navy
  C. War in the North
    1. Three-pronged drive against Canada
    2. Perry's exploits on Lake Erie
    3. Battle of the Thames
  D. Jackson defeats Creeks at Horseshoe Bend, 1814
  E. British efforts in 1814
    1. British war weariness
    2. British lose Battle of Lake Champlain
    3. Invasions of Washington and Baltimore

F. Battle of New Orleans
    1. Efforts of Jackson and Packingham
    2. Significance of the battle
G. Terms of Treaty of Ghent
H. The Hartford Convention
    1. Composition and attitudes
    2. Actions taken
    3. Consequences of the meeting
I. Aftermath of the war
    1. Patriotism and nationalism
    2. Encouragement of transportation and manufacturing
    3. Action against the Barbary pirates
    4. Reversal of roles of the Republicans and Federalists

KEY ITEMS OF CHRONOLOGY

Inauguration of Jefferson	1801
Marbury v. *Madison* decision	1803
Louisiana Purchase	1803
Jefferson reelected	1804
Burr-Hamilton duel	1804
Lewis and Clark expedition	1804–1806
Embargo Act	1807
Slave trade ended	1808
Madison elected	1808
Non-Intercourse Act	1809
Macon's Bill No. 2	1810
War declared	1812
Treaty of Ghent	December 1814
Hartford Convention	December 1814
Washington, D.C., burned	1814
The "Star-Spangled Banner" composed	1814
Battle of New Orleans	January 1815

TERMS TO MASTER

Listed below are some important people or terms with which you should be familiar after your study of the chapter. Identify each name or term.

1. Revolution of 1800
2. *Marbury* v. *Madison*
3. "midnight appointments"
4. Louisiana Purchase
5. Lewis and Clark expedition
6. Essex Junto
7. Burr Conspiracy
8. John Randolph of Roanoke

9. *Tertium Quid*
10. Aaron Burr
11. judicial review
12. executive privilege
13. embargo
14. Non-Intercourse Act
15. Macon's Bill No. 2
16. War Hawks
17. Oliver H. Perry
18. William Henry Harrison
19. Fort McHenry
20. Battle of New Orleans

VOCABULARY BUILDING

Listed below are some words or phrases used in this chapter. Look in the dictionary for the meaning of each term you do not know.

1. cuisine
2. chastise
3. extortion
4. sanction
5. secede
6. dissidents
7. venomous
8. shrill
9. dubious
10. grouse
11. cockeyed
12. stellar
13. indiscreet
14. intractable
15. liable
16. daunting
17. accost
18. revocation
19. maritime
20. brunt

EXERCISES FOR UNDERSTANDING

When you have finished reading the chapter, answer each of the following questions. If you have difficulty, go back to the text and reread the section of the chapter related to the question.

Multiple-Choice Questions

Select the letter of the response that best completes the statement.

1. The Revolution of 1800 involved the
   A. wholesale ouster of Federalists from the government.
   B. shooting death of Alexander Hamilton.
   C. peaceful transfer of power.
   D. defeat of the *Tertium Quid* by Jefferson.

2. The Supreme Court's decision in *Marbury* v. *Madison*
   A. was sparked by Adams's "midnight appointments."
   B. established the Court's power to declare laws unconstitutional.
   C. had no effect on Marbury's appointment.
   D. all of the above

3. In the early 1800s, the chief sources of revenue for the federal government were
   A. taxes on corporations and slaves.
   B. excise and income taxes.
   C. the tariff and western land sales.
   D. property taxes and state assessments.

4. Jefferson's domestic successes included
   A. extending Federalist taxes.
   B. outlawing the slave trade.
   C. eliminating Adams's judicial appointments.
   D. all of the above

5. Aaron Burr
   A. was vice-president of the United States.
   B. was killed by Alexander Hamilton in a duel.
   C. sided with the Essex Junto, which plotted for New England's independence.
   D. all of the above

6. Jefferson's Embargo
   A. caused the British to weaken their policies against the United States.
   B. was developed because of the strength of the United States Navy which would enforce it.
   C. hurt the South more than any other section.
   D. was repealed before Madison took office.

7. At the Battle of Tippecanoe,
   A. Tecumseh's attempt at Indian unity was defeated.
   B. Andrew Jackson won the major battle in the War of 1812.
   C. Oliver H. Perry defeated the British.
   D. Jefferson finally secured possession of Louisiana.

8. The trial of Aaron Burr established the constitutional precedent that
   A. treason covered a broad range of offenses.
   B. the Supreme Court could review the decisions of lower courts.
   C. the executive was independent of the courts.
   D. the Bill of Rights did not apply to criminal trials.

9. The War of 1812
   A. found the U.S. army unready for war.
   B. saw the British gain control of the Great Lakes.
   C. included British occupation and destruction of New Orleans.
   D. encouraged American commitment to be an agricultural nation.

10. The Treaty of Ghent
    A. settled the dispute with the Barbary pirates.
    B. ended the War of 1812.
    C. enabled the United States to buy Louisiana.
    D. secured the West from the Indians.

True-False Questions

Indicate whether each statement is true or false.

1. By 1840, 40 percent of Americans lived west of the Appalachian Mountains.

2. Thomas Jefferson's "midnight appointments" led to *Marbury* v. *Madison.*

3. In purchasing Louisiana, Jefferson worried that the Constitution did not include the power to buy territory.

4. The *Tertium Quid* advocated independence for New England.

5. Congress supported the Lewis and Clark expedition because it would yield vast scientific knowledge of the West

6. Alexander Hamilton killed Aaron Burr in a duel.

7. During the War of 1812, the British captured Washington, D.C.

8. Representatives from farming regions of the South and West advocated war in 1812.

9. The Battle of New Orleans, perhaps the greatest victory of the war, occurred after the peace treaty had been signed.

10. At the Hartford Convention, New England representatives protested the War of 1812.

Essay Questions

1. Was Jefferson a successful president?

2. What were the bases of the division between the Federalists and the Republicans? Which party was victorious in the short term and in the long run?

3. How did differences between the sections of the nation affect national policies during the Jefferson and Madison administrations?

4. What effects did the War of 1812 have on the economy and culture of the United States? Was the war worth the costs?

ANSWERS TO MULTIPLE-CHOICE
AND TRUE-FALSE QUESTIONS

Multiple-Choice Questions

1-C, 2-D, 3-C, 4-A, 5-D, 6-A, 7-A, 8-C, 9-A, 10-B

True-False Questions

1-T, 2-F, 3-T, 4-F, 5-F, 6-F, 7-T, 8-T, 9-T, 10-T

10 ⬯

NATIONALISM AND SECTIONALISM

CHAPTER OBJECTIVES

After you finish reading and studying this chapter, you should be able to

1. Explain the emergence of nationalism after the War of 1812 in the economy, the government, diplomacy, Supreme Court decisions, and politics.

2. Trace the outbursts of sectionalism between 1816 and 1828.

3. Explain the demise of the first political party system and analyze the shifting patterns of party principles in this era.

4. Assess the significant Supreme Court decisions of this time.

5. Account for the political rise of Andrew Jackson.

CHAPTER OUTLINE

I. Development of nationalism
   A. Stages in growth of nationalism
   B. War of 1812 and nationalism

II. Economic nationalism
   A. National Bank
      1. Results of expiration of the national bank in 1811
      2. New Bank of the United States chartered
      3. Debate over Second National Bank
   B. Protective tariff of 1816
   C. Internal improvements
      1. The National Road

    2. Calhoun's proposal
    3. Madison's veto of bill
    4. State and private responsibility

III. "Era of Good Feelings"
  A. James Monroe
    1. His background
    2. Election of 1816
    3. His strict construction of the Constitution
    4. His cabinet
  B. Relative harmony of Monroe administration
  C. Election of 1820 ends first party system
  D. Rapprochement with Britain
    1. Significance of Rush-Bagot Agreement, 1817
    2. Issues settled in Convention of 1818
  E. Significance of the year 1819
  F. Acquisition of Florida
    1. Weakened Spanish control
    2. Jackson's capture of Florida panhandle
    3. Terms of settlement with Spain

IV. Signs of growing political disharmony
  A. Panic of 1819
    1. Causes
    2. Duration
  B. The Missouri Compromise
    1. Slave-state–free-state balance
    2. Debate over Missouri's statehood
    3. Terms of the compromise

V. Supreme Court and judicial nationalism
  A. Assertion of judicial review
    1. *Marbury* v. *Madison* (1803)
    2. *Fletcher* v. *Peck* (1810)
  B. Protection of contract rights in *Dartmouth College* v. *Woodward* (1819)
  C. Curb on state powers in *McCulloch* v. *Maryland* (1819)
  D. National supremacy in commerce, *Gibbons* v. *Ogden* (1824)

VI. Nationalist diplomacy
  A. Negotiating Russia out of Oregon
  B. The Monroe Doctrine
    1. Latin American liberation wars
    2. British efforts in Latin America

3. Assertion of Monroe Doctrine
4. Effects of doctrine
VII. One-party politics
  A. Election of 1824
    1. Candidates and issues
    2. The election is decided in the House
    3. Charges of "Corrupt Bargain"
  B. Presidency of John Quincy Adams
    1. Strong nationalism
    2. Blueprint for development
    3. Mistakes and frustrations
    4. Tariff of 1828
  C. Election of 1828
    1. Opposition to Jackson
    2. Jackson's appeal
    3. Extension of suffrage in the states
    4. Jackson's background
    5. Outcome of election

KEY ITEMS OF CHRONOLOGY

Second National Bank (B.U.S.) chartered	1816
Protective tariff	1816
"Era of Good Feelings"	about 1816–1819
Monroe's administrations	1817–1825
Rush-Bagot Agreement	1817
Acquisition of Florida	1819
Financial panic	1819
Transcontinental Treaty	1819
Dartmouth College v. *Woodward*	1819
McCulloch v. *Maryland*	1819
Monroe elected	1820
Missouri Compromise	1820
Monroe Doctrine	1823
Gibbons v. *Ogden*	1824
John Quincy Adams's administration	1825–1829
Election of Andrew Jackson	1828

TERMS TO MASTER

Listed below are some important people or terms with which you should be familiar after your study of the chapter. Identify each name or term.

1. Bank of the United States
2. "Era of Good Feelings"
3. John C. Calhoun
4. James Monroe
5. internal improvements
6. Daniel Webster
7. John C. Calhoun
8. James Monroe
9. Henry Clay
10. Tallmadge amendment
11. John Marshall
12. judicial review
13. *Dartmouth College* v. *Woodward*
14. *McCulloch* v. *Maryland*
15. *Gibbons* v. *Ogden*
16. Monroe Doctrine
17. "corrupt bargain"
18. John Quincy Adams
19. Tariff of 1824
20. *South Carolina Exposition and Protest*
21. Rachel Jackson

VOCABULARY BUILDING

Listed below are some words or phrases used in this chapter. Look in the dictionary for the meaning of each term you do not know.

1. dispersion
2. strident
3. trinity
4. alignment
5. triumvirate
6. spawn
7. maxim
8. rancorous
9. tenacity
10. panhandle (n.)
11. affirm
12. sage
13. unilateral
14. treachery
15. chronic
16. obstinant
17. ruse
18. chagrin
19. mudslinging
20. plumb

EXERCISES FOR UNDERSTANDING

When you have finished reading the chapter, answer each of the following questions. If you have difficulty, go back to the text and reread the section of the chapter related to the question.

Multiple-Choice Questions

Select the letter of the response that best completes the statement.

1. In the 1810s John C. Calhoun was
   A. more nationalistic than he was later.
   B. a stronger advocate of states' rights than he was in the 1830s.
   C. the same as he was later—his positions did not change.
   D. in complete agreement with Daniel Webster.

2. The "Era of Good Feelings" described
   A. John Marshall's tenure on the Supreme Court.
   B. the administration of James Monroe.
   C. the administration of John Quincy Adams.
   D. the 1820s.

3. The last of the Revolutionary generation to be president was
   A. James Madison.
   B. James Monroe.
   C. John Quincy Adams.
   D. Andrew Jackson.

4. John Marshall and the Supreme Court upheld the "implied powers" of Congress and the supremacy of the national government in
   A. *Marbury* v. *Madison.*
   B. *Dartmouth* v. *Woodward.*
   C. *McCulloch* v. *Maryland.*
   D. *Gibbons* v. *Ogden.*

5. When Thomas Jefferson said that "this momentous question like a firebell in the night awakened and filled me with terror. I considered it at once the knell of the Union," he referred to the
   A. corruption in the election of 1824.
   B. controversy over slavery in the territories.
   C. debate over the Bank of the United States.
   D. role of the federal government in internal improvement.

6. The Missouri Compromise of 1820
   A. outlawed the foreign slave trade and declared slavery an evil.
   B. banned slavery from all of the Louisiana Purchase territory.
   C. ended the slave-state–free-state balance in the U.S. Senate.
   D. admitted Missouri as a slave state.

7. In settling the northwestern boundary of the United States, Secretary of State Adams had to negotiate with
   A. Russia.
   B. Spain.
   C. Canada.
   D. the Indians.

8. The Monroe Doctrine
   A. was issued jointly with Great Britain.
   B. brought a storm of protest from other nations.
   C. gave the United States control over internal affairs in Latin America.
   D. promised that the United States would not interfere with existing European colonies.

9. As a result of the "corrupt bargain,"
   A. Henry Clay's American System suffered a crushing defeat.
   B. John Quincy Adams became president.
   C. the Bank of the United States was established.
   D. Congress approved the Monroe Doctrine.

10. The presidential candidates in the 1828 campaign
   A. concentrated almost exclusively on the issues of internal improvements and the national bank.
   B. thoroughly debated the theories of nationalism.
   C. focused discussions entirely on the tariff and foreign affairs.
   D. engaged in personal attacks.

True-False Questions

Indicate whether each statement is true or false.

1. Jefferson, Madison, and Monroe all encouraged a constitutional amendment to ensure that Congress had the power to enact internal improvements.

2. The financial Panic of 1819 was one indicator that the Era of Good Feelings was ending.

3. In 1818 Andrew Jackson and John C. Calhoun disagreed over Indian policy in Oregon.

4. In 1819, Spain gave Florida to the United States.

5. President Monroe supported the "new nationalism," including internal improvements.

6. The House of Representatives elected John Quincy Adams president.

7. The "corrupt bargain" referred to the Marshall court's decision in *Gibbons* v. *Ogden.*

8. As president, John Quincy Adams was a strong nationalist.

9. John C. Calhoun supported protective tariffs in 1816 and 1824.

10. In 1828 Daniel Webster proposed that a state could nullify an act of Congress.

Essay Questions

1. Explain the problems the United States encountered with Britain, Spain, and Russia between 1815 and 1828 and how those issues were resolved.

2. How did the Supreme Court contribute to the growing nationalism of the early nineteenth century? Cite specific cases as examples.

3. Who were the major national political figures between the War of 1812 and the election of Andrew Jackson? How and why did their alliances and coalitions shift during this period?

4. Of Madison, Monroe, and John Quincy Adams, who was the most and the least successful president? Why?

5. What were the provisions of the Missouri Compromise, and what did it accomplish?

6. What personal and political factors led to the election of Andrew Jackson in 1828?

ANSWERS TO MULTIPLE-CHOICE AND TRUE-FALSE QUESTIONS

Multiple-Choice Questions

1-A, 2-B, 3-B, 4-C, 5-B, 6-D, 7-A, 8-D, 9-B, 10-D

True-False Questions

1-T, 2-T, 3-F, 4-T, 5-F, 6-T, 7-F, 8-T, 9-F, 10-F

11 ∽

THE JACKSONIAN IMPULSE

CHAPTER OBJECTIVES

After you finish reading and studying this chapter, you should be able to

1. Explain the political controversy between Jackson and Calhoun.

2. Understand and explain the nullification controversy with South Carolina.

3. Understand and explain the bank war and its economic consequences.

4. Evaluate Jackson's Indian policy.

5. Analyze and explain the emergence of the second political party system.

6. Assess the significance of Jacksonian democracy.

CHAPTER OUTLINE

I. New Political Culture
   A. Mass politics
      1. Easing voting restrictions
      2. Common-man politician
   B. Political parties
      1. Stands on issues
      2. Nominating conventions
      3. Party machines
   C. Elite control

II. Jackson takes office
   A. Inauguration
   B. Political appointments

    C. Calhoun-Van Buren rivalry
        1. Peggy Eaton affair
        2. Internal improvements
          a. Maysville Road Bill
          b. Jackson's veto

III. Nullification issue and crisis
    A. Situation in Calhoun's South Carolina
    B. Calhoun's theory of nullification
        1. Abandons nationalism
        2. *South Carolina Exposition and Protest*
    C. The Webster-Hayne Debate
        1. Initial issue of western lands
        2. States' rights vs. nationalism
        3. Impact of the dispute
    D. Break with Calhoun
        1. Jefferson Day Dinner
          a. Jackson's toast
          b. Calhoun's response
        2. Revelation of Calhoun's 1818 view of Jackson
        3. Changes in cabinet
        4. Appointment of Van Buren
        5. Calhoun's reaction
    E. Nullification crisis
        1. South Carolina's actions
          a. Nullification ordinance
          b. Reactions
        2. Jackson asks for Force Bill
        3. Calhoun opposes secession
        4. Clay's Compromise approved
        5. South Carolina rescinds nullification

IV. Racial prejudice in Jacksonian era
    A. Equality versus white supremacy
    B. Attitudes toward blacks
        1. Treatment of northern free blacks
          a. Segregation
          b. Anti-black riots
        2. Southern slavery
    C. Jackson's Indian policy
        1. Jackson's attitude
        2. Indian removal treaties negotiated
        3. The Black Hawk War and other resistance
        4. Cherokee "Trail of Tears"
          a. Background to the Georgia actions

      b. Supreme Court rulings
      c. Jackson's reaction
      d. Cherokee removal

V. The bank controversy
  A. Opposition of the bank
  B. Contributions of the bank
  C. The effort to recharter
    1. Biddle's plan
    2. Impact of Jackson's veto

VI. The election of 1832
  A. Innovations
    1. Rise of the Anti-Masonic party
    2. Use of national conventions
  B. Results of the election

VII. Jackson's renewed war on the B.U.S.
  A. Removal of deposits
  B. Use of "pet banks"
  C. Economic impact of the changes
    1. B.U.S. tightening of credit
    2. Speculative binge
    3. Increase in land sales
    4. Increases in state debts
  D. Deflation
    1. Terms and impact of the Distribution Act
    2. Importance of the Specie Circular
    3. International complications

VIII. The new party system
  A. The Whig party
    1. Sources of support
    2. Whig philosophy
  B. The election of 1836
    1. Nature of the contest
    2. Results

IX. The Van Buren's administration
  A. Van Buren's background
  B. The Panic of 1837
    1. Causes and effects
    2. Van Buren's attitude and actions
  C. Creation of the Independent Treasury
    1. Whigs and economic development

    2. Passage in 1840
  D. Other issues of the time

X. The election of 1840
  A. Parties and candidates
  B. Nature of the campaign
  C. Outcome

XI. Assessing the Jackson years
  A. Development of political parties
  B. Conflicting interpretations of Jackson
  C. Consequences of Jackson's laissez-faire policies

KEY ITEMS OF CHRONOLOGY

Calhoun's *Exposition and Protest*	1828
Jackson's administrations	1829–1837
Veto of the Maysville Road Bill	1830
Webster-Hayne Debate	1830
Indian Removal Act	1830
Veto of bank recharter	1832
Worcester v. *Georgia*	1832
Black Hawk War	1832
South Carolina ordinance of nullification	1832
Nullification Proclamation	1832
Reelection of Andrew Jackson	1832
Force Bill and Compromise Tariff	1833
Cherokee Treaty and the "Trail of Tears"	1835–1838
Distribution Act and Specie Circular	1836
Panic of 1837	1837
Van Buren's administration	1837–1841
Independent Treasury passed	1840
"Log Cabin and Hard Cider" campaign	1840
Election of William Henry Harrison	1840

TERMS TO MASTER

Listed below are some important people or terms with which you should be familiar after your study of the chapter. Identify each name or term.

1. "age of the common man"
2. spoils system
3. Martin Van Buren
4. Peggy Eaton
5. John C. Calhoun
6. Maysville Road Bill
7. nullification
8. Tariff of Abominations
9. *South Carolina Exposition and Protest*
10. Webster-Hayne Debate
11. "Trail of Tears"
12. Daniel Webster
13. Nullification Proclamation
14. Henry Clay
15. Force Bill
16. *Worcester* v. *Georgia*
17. Nicholas Biddle
18. Bank of the United States
19. Anti-Masonic party
20. "pet banks"
21. Distribution Act
22. Whigs
23. Independent Treasury
24. "Log Cabin and Hard Cider Campaign"
25. William Henry Harrison

VOCABULARY BUILDING

Listed below are some words or phrases used in this chapter. Look in the dictionary for the meaning of each term you do not know.

1. subservient
2. polemic
3. succulent
4. rebuke
5. secede
6. rash (adj.)
7. subjugation
8. degrade
9. cede
10. ponder
11. disburse
12. summarily
13. censure
14. precarious
15. bonanza
16. remnants
17. savvy
18. rally (v.)
19. sardonic
20. commodious

EXERCISES FOR UNDERSTANDING

When you have finished reading the chapter, answer each of the following questions. If you have difficulty, go back to the text and reread the section of the chapter related to the question.

Multiple-Choice Questions

Select the letter of the response that best completes the statement.

1. In the early nineteenth century,
   A. women finally got the right to vote.
   B. the percentage of people voting shrank because of the influx of immigrants who could not qualify to vote.
   C. many states dropped property requirements for voting.
   D. qualifications for voting remained unchanged.

2. The two main rivals in the Jackson administration were
   A. Martin Van Buren and Daniel Webster.
   B. Henry Clay and John C. Calhoun.
   C. Nicholas Biddle and Henry Clay.
   D. Martin Van Buren and John C. Calhoun.

3. In dealing with internal improvements, Andrew Jackson
   A. opposed all federal financing of roads, bridges, and railroads.
   B. wanted federal aid only for local projects.
   C. supported federal funds only for interstate programs.
   D. approved all expenditures passed by Congress.

4. John C. Calhoun's theory of nullification provided
   A. encouragement for secession from the Union.
   B. that the United States Supreme Court could overrule a state's nullification.
   C. that states had the right to "nullify" specific pieces of federal legislation.
   D. a satisfactory compromise between his views and the position of Jackson.

5. The immediate issue that spurred the Webster-Hayne debate was the
   A. expansion of slavery.
   B. protective tariff.
   C. sale of western lands.
   D. financing of internal improvements.

6. Jackson's action in regard to the Indians was to
   A. oppose their removal to the West.
   B. refuse to enforce a Supreme Court decision in the Indians' favor.
   C. defend Indian rights to disputed lands in Georgia.
   D. send troops to slaughter the Indians.

7. In the Jacksonian era, free blacks in the North
   A. had the right to vote but encountered personal discrimination.
   B. were denied civil rights but were integrated in society.
   C. were all sent to the free territories in the West.
   D. experienced pervasive discrimination and segregation.

8. Jackson helped to bring an early end to the Bank of the United States by
   A. suing the bank in federal court.
   B. beginning to deposit government funds in state banks rather than in the Bank of the United States.
   C. getting Congress to pass an act killing the bank.
   D. persuading the English to withdraw their funds from the bank.

9. To keep the government financially sound after the panic of 1837, Van Buren proposed
   A. reviving the Bank of the United States.
   B. government aid to state banks.
   C. an Independent Treasury.
   D. a higher tariff and an increase in the money supply.

10. The Whig party developed in opposition to
    A. John Quincy Adams, Henry Clay, and Daniel Webster.
    B. Jacksonian Democrats.
    C. slavery and the Bank of the United States.
    D. all of the above

True-False Questions

Indicate whether each statement is true or false.

1. The "Eaton malaria" united Van Buren and Calhoun.

2. To defend nullification, Calhoun resigned as vice-president.

3. In the Webster-Hayne debate, Webster managed to subtly drive a wedge between the South and the West in Congress.

4. Daniel Webster said, "Liberty and Union, now and forever, one and inseparable."

5. In *Worcester* v. *Georgia,* the Supreme Court ruled that Georgia law did not apply to the Cherokee nation.

6. Resistance to the Indian Removal Act came largely from northern tribes.

7. The first third party in American presidential politics was the Anti-Masonic party.

8. Depositing federal funds in "pet banks" helped to stop the mania of speculation in the nation in 1836 and 1837.

9. Martin Van Buren was known as the "Little Magician" and the "Red Fox."

10. In 1840, William Henry Harrison campaigned as a strong supporter of internal improvement and a national bank.

Essay Questions

1. What was different about the political culture of the Jacksonian period? How did these new characteristics contribute to Jackson's success?

2. What was the nullification crisis all about and why was it important?

3. Compare and contrast the treatment of blacks and Indians in the Jacksonian era.

4. Why was the Bank of the United States so controversial? Assess the opposing positions on the B.U.S.

5. How did the presidential elections of 1832, 1836, and 1840 resemble each other and how did they differ?

6. Was Jackson a successful president? Explain.

ANSWERS TO MULTIPLE-CHOICE AND TRUE-FALSE QUESTIONS

Multiple-Choice Questions

1-C, 2-D, 3-C, 4-C, 5-C, 6-B, 7-D, 8-B, 9-C, 10-B

True-False Questions

1-F, 2-T, 3-T, 4-T, 5-T, 6-F, 7-T, 8-F, 9-T, 10-F

12 ⌬

THE DYNAMICS OF GROWTH

CHAPTER OBJECTIVES

After you finish reading and studying this chapter, you should be able to

1. Explain changes in agriculture from 1800 to 1860 and describe their social and economic impact.

2. List and describe improvements in transportation and communication from 1800 to 1860.

3. Analyze the significant advances in technology from 1800 to 1860 and their impact on society.

4. Account for the emergence of the factory as a method of production and assess its social impact.

5. Explain how the growth of manufacturing affected urbanization and vice versa.

6. Appreciate the changes in popular culture during this period.

7. Describe the nature of immigration prior to 1860 and the reaction of previously settled Americans to this new immigration.

8. Analyze the early development of labor unions and account for their failure to gain widespread acceptance.

9. Describe and explain the distribution of wealth in the United States in "the era of the common man."

10. Explain the rise of the major professions in the decades before the Civil War.

CHAPTER OUTLINE

I. National agriculture
   A. The importance of southern cotton
      1. Invention of the cotton gin
      2. Revolutionary impact of the cotton gin
         a. Effects on slavery
         b. Spurs westward migration
         c. Increases cotton exports
   B. The westward movement
      1. Nature of the movement
      2. Incentives to move west
         a. Soil exhaustion
         b. Improved plows
         c. Effects of new land laws

II. Developments in transportation and communication
   A. Road improvements
   B. Water transportation
      1. Flatboats
      2. Steamboats
      3. Canals
   C. Railroads
      1. Mania for railroads
      2. Problems with rail transport
      3. Advantages of rail transport
      4. Effects of railroad growth
   D. Ocean transport
      1. Transatlantic packet service
      2. The brief era of clipper ships
   E. Government involvement in transportation improvement
   F. Communications revolution
      1. Telegraph
      2. Mail "express"

III. Growth of industry
   A. Impact of technology
   B. Textile manufacturing
      1. Early handicraft system
      2. Basis of British lead
      3. Early American textile factories
   C. Technological improvements
      1. McCormick reaper
      2. Vulcanizing rubber

        3. Telegraph
        4. Widespread impact of other technological changes
    D. The Lowell factory system
        1. Basic features of the system
        2. Importance of paternal supervision of female workers
        3. Spread and transformation of the system
    E. Contrasts of the family system
    F. Growth of cities

IV. Popular culture
    A. Urban recreation
        1. Drinking
        2. Fraternal societies, lectures, circuses
        3. Blood sports
    B. Theater
    C. Minstrel shows

V. Immigration
    A. The need for labor
    B. Increases in immigration
    C. Changes in handling new immigrants
    D. The Irish immigration
        1. Reasons for emigrating
        2. Growth of Irish immigration
        3. Background and demography
        4. Areas of settlement
        5. Level of misery
        6. Irish success stories
        7. Strong anti-Irish attitudes
        8. Irish political involvement
        9. Linkage to the Catholic church
    E. German immigration
        1. Periods of high immigration
        2. Background and method of immigration
        3. German success stories
    F. Other groups
        1. British and Scandinavian immigrants
        2. Immigration from China
    G. Nativist reaction to immigration
        1. Causes of antagonism to immigrants
        2. Evidences of nativist activity
        3. Rise of the Know-Nothing Party
    H. Immigrant makeup of the labor force

VI. Work, organized labor, and the professions
    A. Skilled work in Revolutionary era

1. Hierarchy of guild system
2. Daily routine
3. Trade associations
4. Use of slaves

B. Organized labor
   1. Early labor unions
   2. Impact of the Massachusetts decision *Commonwealth* v. *Hunt* (1842)

C. Involvement of labor in politics
   1. Nature of Working Men's parties
   2. Evolution into Locofocos or Equal Rights party
   3. Impact of labor parties on politics

D. Rise of professions
   1. Specialized knowledge and skills
   2. Diversified workforce
   3. Reading revolution
   4. Specific professions
      a. Teaching
      b. The law
      c. Medicine
      d. Engineering
   5. Women
      a. Nursing and teaching
      b. Religious and benevolent work

VII. Social stratification in the Jacksonian era
   A. Evidence of widening gap between rich and poor
   B. Probing waves and causes of social stratification
   C. American white population compared with Europe's

KEY ITEMS OF CHRONOLOGY

Eli Whitney invented the cotton gin	1793
Wilderness Road opened	1795
Fulton's steamboat sails up Hudson River	1807
First factory founded at Waltham, Mass.	1813
Opening of the Erie Canal	1825
John Deere invents steel plow	1837
Cyrus McCormick patented the mechanical reaper	1841
Commonwealth v. *Hunt*	1842
Charles Goodyear patented the vulcanizing process	1844
Know-Nothing Party established	1854

TERMS TO MASTER

Listed below are some important people or terms with which you should be familiar after your study of the chapter. Identify each name or term.

1. Eli Whitney
2. cotton gin
3. John Deere
4. Preemption Act of 1830
5. Wilderness Road
6. turnpikes
7. steamboats
8. Robert Fulton
9. Erie Canal
10. Cyrus McCormick
11. Samuel F. B. Morse
12. Lowell system
13. minstrel show
14. nativism
15. Know-Nothing Party
16. *Commonwealth* v. *Hunt*
17. "literacy revolution"
18. John Jacob Astor

VOCABULARY BUILDING

Listed below are some words or phrases used in this chapter. Look in the dictionary for the meaning of each term you do not know.

1. proliferate
2. leached
3. emigrants
4. mania
5. tributary
6. epic
7. oblivious
8. spate
9. dexterity
10. pervasive
11. melodrama
12. minstrels
13. raucous
14. arbiter
15. blissful
16. apprentice
17. solicitude
18. garner
19. antebellum
20. lax

EXERCISES FOR UNDERSTANDING

When you have finished reading the chapter, answer each of the following questions. If you have difficulty, go back to the text and reread the section of the chapter related to the question.

Multiple-Choice Questions

Select the letter of the response that best completes the statement.

1. The most important American export in the 1830s and 1840s was
   A. farm equipment.
   B. textiles.
   C. cotton.
   D. railroad cars and engines.

2. Developments in transportation usually occurred in the following order:
   A. railroads, flatboats, canals, and turnpikes.
   B. turnpikes, steamboats, canals, and railroads.
   C. turnpikes, canals, flatboats, and steamboats.
   D. canals, turnpikes, railroads, and steamboats.

3. Most financing for railroads came from
   A. private corporations.
   B. the federal government.
   C. state and local governments.
   D. foreign investors.

4. A uniquely American form of mass entertainment was
   A. bare-knuckle prizefighting.
   B. the circus.
   C. cockfighting.
   D. the minstrel show.

5. In 1860, the largest immigrant group in the United States was the
   A. Germans.
   B. British.
   C. Italians.
   D. Irish.

6. Most workers in the Lowell textile mills were
   A. slaves.
   B. entire families.
   C. single women.
   D. immigrants, especially Irish and Germans.

7. One reason factories appeared first in New England was that
   A. the region had failed to succeed in other commercial activities.
   B. the states supported early manufacturing with subsidies.
   C. its slaves had little cotton to pick and could work in factories.
   D. the profits from the region's trade provided the needed capital to invest.

8. The cause of Irish emigration was *not*
   A. persecution by the British landlords.
   B. British hostility to their Protestant religion.
   C. an epidemic of potato rot.
   D. the great population density and a prolonged depression in Ireland.

9. Labor unions in the late 1820s and 1830s
   A. experienced some national organization.
   B. spent most of their energy on the creation of Working Men's parties.
   C. attracted most of the laboring people into their membership.
   D. were open to all workers, not simply those who pursued a special craft.

10. The profession of engineering developed largely as a result of
    A. the immigration of German intellectuals.
    B. the physical and industrial expansion of the nation.
    C. the development of railroads.
    D. John Jacob Astor's founding of the Massachusetts Institute of Technology.

True-False Questions

Indicate whether each statement is true or false.

1. The Preemption Act of 1830 made land available for the construction of canals.

2. The Erie Canal, in effect, joined the Great Lakes to Boston.

3. The invention of the steel plow was to the West what the cotton gin was to the South.

4. Railroads aided the expansion of manufacturing more than farming.

5. The sewing machine was a great boost to the growth of textile factories.

6. The drinking culture of the 1830s primarily involved the working class.

7. The influx of German immigrants in the 1850s included many learned, cultured, professional people.

8. Before the Civil War, affluent homes in America had such luxuries as indoor plumbing, central heating, bathtubs, sewing machines, and iceboxes.

9. In *Commonwealth* v. *Hunt,* the Supreme Court ruled all labor unions illegal.

10. Labor activists in the 1830s promoted the ten-hour work day.

Essay Questions

1. How did changes in technology and transportation affect American agriculture?

2. Compare and contrast the effects of changes in water transportation and the development of the railroad.

3. What forms of entertainment became popular in the rapidly growing urban areas?

4. Explain the position of labor unions in American society during the antebellum period and illustrate how they contributed to society.

5. Describe the immigrants who came to the United States between 1830 and 1860 and explain the reaction to them.

6. Assess the accuracy of the term "the age of the common man" in describing the antebellum period.

ANSWERS TO MULTIPLE-CHOICE AND TRUE-FALSE QUESTIONS

Multiple-Choice Questions

1-C, 2-B, 3-A, 4-D, 5-D, 6-C, 7-D, 8-D, 9-A, 10-B

True-False Questions

1-F, 2-F, 3-T, 4-F, 5-F, 6-F, 7-T, 8-T, 9-F, 10-T

13 ∽

AN AMERICAN RENAISSANCE:
RELIGION, ROMANTICISM, AND REFORM

CHAPTER OBJECTIVES

After you finish reading and studying this chapter, you should be able to

1. Describe the religious denominations developed after the Enlightenment.

2. Account for the Second Great Awakening and trace its impact on society.

3. Understand the nature of Transcendentalism and describe its impact on the intellectual life of the United States.

4. Appreciate the major literary figures of the antebellum period and portray their contributions.

5. Assess the stirrings for improvement in education.

6. Explain the impetus for reform and show its manifestations in temperance, prisons, asylums, and women's rights.

7. Account for the movement for utopian communities and describe significant examples.

CHAPTER OUTLINE

   I. The Enlightenment's impact on nineteenth-century America
     A. Sense of mission for the nation
     B. Three rational religious concepts
        1. Deism
           a. Optimistic religious outlook
           b. Concept of God's role
           c. Impact on Protestantism

       2. Unitarianism
         a. Basic concepts
         b. Breadth of its impact
       3. Universalism
         a. Groups to which it appealed
         b. Basic tenets

II. The Second Great Awakening
   A. Frontier phase
       1. Advent of the camp meeting
       2. Audience to which the movement appealed
       3. The Baptists
         a. Emphasis and appeals of the Baptists
         b. Nature of Baptist organization
       4. The Methodists
         a. More centralized organization
         b. Role of the circuit riders
       5. Nature of the camp meetings
   B. The "Burned-Over District"
       1. Role of Charles G. Finney
       2. Finney's message
       3. Nature of Oberlin College

III. The Mormons
   A. The origins of the sect
   B. Nature of organization and beliefs
   C. Brigham Young and the move to Utah
   D. Fate of the State of Deseret

IV. Romanticism in America
   A. The emphasis of the romantic movement
   B. Transcendentalism
       1. Origins of the movement and nature of beliefs
       2. Development of Ralph Waldo Emerson's interest in Transcendentalism
       3. Henry David Thoreau
         a. Thoreau's interests and ideas
         b. Thoreau's life at Walden Pond
         c. Basis and message of his essay "Civil Disobedience"
       4. The impact of the movement

V. The flowering of American literature
   A. Emily Dickinson's work and role
   B. Nathaniel Hawthorne's contributions
   C. Edgar Allan Poe evaluated

      D. Herman Melville
          1. His background
          2. The significance of *Moby-Dick*
      E. The controversial role of Walt Whitman
      F. The popular press
          1. Technological advances
          2. Cheap newspapers, magazines, and books
          3. Contributions of the *New York Herald* and *Tribune*

  VI. Education
      A. Level of literacy
      B. Growth of the public schools
          1. Need for a literate electorate
          2. Horace Mann's contributions
          3. Education in the South
          4. Teaching as a career
          5. Private academies
      C. Higher education
          1. A surge of colleges and state universities
          2. Conflicts over funding and curricula
      D. Education for women
          1. Level of schools
          2. Divergence from men's education

 VII. Reform movements
      A. Roots of reform
      B. Varieties of reform
      C. Temperance
          1. Rate of alcohol consumption
          2. Arguments for temperance
          3. Organizations for temperance
          4. Debates over goals and methods
      D. Prison reform
          1. Optimism breeds new approaches to punishment
          2. Changing views of prisons
          3. Nature of the Auburn Penitentiary
      E. Treatment of the insane
          1. Early treatment of the insane
          2. Role of Dorothea Dix
      F. Women's rights
          1. Catharine Beecher and the "cult of domesticity"
          2. Status of women in the antebellum period
          3. Significance of the Seneca Falls Convention
          4. Successes of the women's movement

     5. Jobs for educated women
- G. Utopian communities
  1. Bases for their popularity
  2. Concepts of the Shakers
  3. The Oneida Community
     - a. Background of John Humphrey Noyes
     - b. Concept of complex marriage
     - c. Activities and contributions of the community
     - d. Causes for decline and transformation
  4. New Harmony
     - a. Background of Robert Owen
     - b. Principles for his cooperative
     - c. Causes of decline
  5. Brook Farm
     - a. Significant supporters
     - b. Reasons for success
     - c. Dissolution
  6. Evaluation of the utopian communities
- H. Reformers' concern about slavery

KEY ITEMS OF CHRONOLOGY

Second Great Awakening begins	1800
First free public secondary school opened	1821
American Unitarian Association formed	1826
Mormon church founded	1830
American Temperance Society founded	1833
American Temperance Union formed	1833
Emerson's "The American Scholar"	1837
Mormons arrived at Salt Lake	1847
Seneca Falls Convention on women's rights	1848
Oneida Community started	1848
Thoreau's "Civil Disobedience"	1849
Hawthorne's *The Scarlet Letter*	1850
Melville's *Moby-Dick*	1851
Thoreau's *Walden*	1854
Whitman's *Leaves of Grass*	1855

TERMS TO MASTER

Listed below are some important people or terms with which you should be familiar after your study of the chapter. Identify each name or term.

1. deism
2. Unitarianism
3. Universalism
4. Second Great Awakening
5. Charles Grandison Finney
6. Mormons
7. Brigham Young
8. romanticism
9. Transcendentalism
10. Ralph Waldo Emerson
11. Henry David Thoreau
12. *Walden, or Life in the Woods*
13. "Civil Disobedience"
14. Emily Dickinson
15. Nathaniel Hawthorne
16. Edgar Allan Poe
17. Herman Melville
18. Walt Whitman
19. Horace Greeley
20. Horace Mann
21. Oberlin College
22. temperance
23. Dorothea Lynde Dix
24. "cult of domesticity"
25. Lucretia Mott
26. Elizabeth Cady Stanton
27. Margaret Fuller
28. utopian community
29. Oneida Community
30. New Harmony
31. Brook Farm
32. Shakers
33. John Humphrey Noyes
34. phalanxes

VOCABULARY BUILDING

Listed below are some words or phrases used in this chapter. Look in the dictionary for the meaning of each term you do not know.

1. errant
2. swaddled
3. depravity
4. evangelical
5. redemption
6. cataleptic
7. ecumenical
8. spawn
9. unregenerate
10. theology
11. charismatic
12. gentiles
13. arduous
14. affinity
15. uncouth
16. eke
17. lyceum
18. sottish
19. tippling
20. penitence

EXERCISES FOR UNDERSTANDING

When you have finished reading the chapter, answer each of the following questions. If you have difficulty, go back to the text and reread the section of the chapter related to the question.

Multiple-Choice Questions

Select the letter of the response that best completes the statement.

1. Belief in the benevolence of God, the inherent goodness of mankind, and the primacy of reason characterized
   A. the Second Great Awakening.
   B. Romanticism.
   C. Unitarianism.
   D. the writings of Herman Melville.

2. A major force in the Second Great Awakening was
   A. Ralph Waldo Emerson.
   B. Charles Grandison Finney.
   C. John Humphrey Noyes.
   D. William Ellery Channing.

3. The most important new religious group to arise from the Burned-Over District was the
   A. Mormons.
   B. Unitarians-Universalists.
   C. Transcendentalists.
   D. Baptists.

4. "If the law is of such a nature that it requires you to be an agent of unjustice to another, then, I say, break the law," said
   A. Ralph Waldo Emerson.
   B. Edgar Allan Poe.
   C. Henry David Thoreau.
   D. Walt Whitman.

5. American Romanticism
   A. closely resembled the Enlightenment.
   B. showed little interest in the Middle Ages.
   C. emphasized the common man's virtue.
   D. all of the above

6. Horace Mann was a leader in
   A. the "penny" press.
   B. education reform.
   C. the New England literary renaissance.
   D. the Second Great Awakening.

7. Prison reformers wanted prisons to
   A. punish prisoners severely.
   B. rehabilitate prisoners.
   C. permanently remove criminals from society.
   D. make a substantial profit.

8. The organized movement for women's rights had its origins in
   A. the Second Great Awakening.
   B. the lyceum movement.
   C. Transcendentalism.
   D. a split in the antislavery movement.

9. The first convention of women's rights advocates occurred at
   A. Brook Farm.
   B. Walden.
   C. Seneca Falls.
   D. Oneida.

10. Robert Owen started New Harmony, a utopian community based on
    A. Enlightenment rationalism.
    B. the idea that grace was a gift of God.
    C. "complex marriage" and socialism.
    D. strict celibacy and common property.

True-False Questions

Indicate whether each statement is true or false.

1. Deists accepted every statement of the Bible as literally true.

2. Joseph Smith founded the Church of Jesus Christ of Latter-day Saints.

3. Two of the greatest means of spreading the Second Great Awakening on the frontier were the camp meeting and the circuit riders.

4. "If a man does not keep pace with his companion, perhaps it is because he hears a different drummer," wrote Ralph Waldo Emerson.

5. The author of *Leaves of Grass* was Walt Whitman.

6. Horace Greeley originated the "penny" press that emphasized sex, crime, and scandal.

7. The most important antebellum journalist was Horace Greeley.

8. In the nineteenth century Americans had the highest literacy rate in the Western world.

9. Women students at Oberlin College were treated with full equality with male students.

10. Brook Farm stressed the rehabilitation of prisoners.

Essay Questions

1. How were Unitarianism and Universalism rooted in both the Enlightenment and Puritanism? Compare the two religious views.

2. What caused the Second Great Awakening and what changes did it bring to organized society?

3. Who were the major writers of the antebellum period and how did they contribute to a distinctive American literary culture?

4. How did the Second Great Awakening resemble the romantic movement in literature? How did they differ?

5. Of the major antebellum reform movements, which was the most successful and which was the least? Why?

6. What were the major efforts at utopian communities, and why did so many emerge between 1820 and 1860?

ANSWERS TO MULTIPLE-CHOICE AND TRUE-FALSE QUESTIONS

Multiple-Choice Questions

1-C, 2-B, 3-A, 4-C, 5-D, 6-B, 7-B, 8-D, 9-C, 10-A

True-False Questions

1-F, 2-T, 3-T, 4-F, 5-T, 6-F, 7-T, 8-T, 9-F, 10-F

14 ∞

MANIFEST DESTINY

CHAPTER OBJECTIVES

After you finish reading and studying this chapter, you should be able to

1. Account for Tyler's difficulties with Congress and explain the accomplishments of his administration.

2. Explain the issues settled in the Webster-Ashburton Treaty and account for its compromises.

3. Describe the westward surge and trace the impact of settlement in Oregon, California, and Utah.

4. Explain how the annexation of Texas developed.

5. Account for the acquisition of a clear claim to Oregon.

6. Analyze the responsibility for starting the Mexican War and describe its results.

CHAPTER OUTLINE

  I. The Tyler years
    A. Harrison's brief beginning
    B. Tyler's position on issues
    C. Domestic issues
      1. The clash between Clay and Tyler
      2. Tyler left without a party
    D. Foreign affairs
      1. Conflicts between Britain and the United States

      2. Settlements in the Webster-Ashburton Treaty

II. Westward expansion
  A. Manifest Destiny
  B. Indian cultures of the West
     1. Nomadic hunters of the plains
     2. Farmers of the Southwest
     3. Other tribes
     4. Impact of white expansion
  C. The Spanish Southwest
     1. Spanish influences
     2. Mexican revolution
        a. Events in Europe
        b. Mexican independence
  D. The Northwest
     1. The fur trade
     2. Settlement in Oregon
  E. California
     1. Spanish settlement
     2. The Franciscan missions
        a. Relations with Indians
           i. Control
           ii. Conversion
        b. Labor
           i. Indians
           ii. Use of force
           iii. Rebellions

III. Movement west
  A. Trails west
     1. Santa Fe Trail
     2. Overland Trail
  B. Effects of journey west
     1. Hardships, work, disease
     2. Impact on Indians
  C. Donner Party
     1. Origins
     2. Mistakes
     3. Tragedy
  D. John C. Frémont

IV. Involvements in Texas
  A. Settlements
     1. Stephen F. Austin
     2. Cotton
  B. Growing conflict

          1. Mexican opposition
          2. Demands for representation
          3. Santa Anna takes power
          4. Rebellion in Texas
     C. War for independence
          1. Battle of the Alamo
          2. Sam Houston
          3. Capture of Santa Anna
          4. Texas Republic
     D. Attempts to join the United States

   V. Presidency of Polk
     A. Election of 1844
          1. Positions on Texas
          2. Polk's victory
     B. Polk's background
     C. Polk's program
          1. Proslavery stance
          2. Reduction in tariff
          3. Independent Treasury
          4. Geographic expansion
              a. Annexation of Texas
              b. Acquisition of Oregon

  VI. The Mexican War
     A. Disputes with Mexico
     B. Polk's provocation of an attack
     C. Opposition to the war
     D. Preparation for war
          1. Military units compared
          2. Nature of the warfare
          3. Development of a plan of action
          4. Selection of a commander
          5. The character of Zachary Taylor
     E. Annexation of California
          1. Creation of the Republic of California
          2. Steps to conquest by the United States
     F. Taylor's battles
          1. Conquest of Monterey
          2. Polk's suspicions and intrigue
          3. Battle of Buena Vista
     G. Scott's conquest of Mexico City
          1. Amphibious attack on Vera Cruz
          2. Maneuvering to Mexico City

H. Terms of the Treaty of Guadalupe Hidalgo
I. The war's legacy
   1. Human and financial costs
   2. Territory acquired
   3. A cluster of military firsts
   4. Impact on the nation
     a. Initial pride
     b. Failure to become a national legend
     c. Individuals promoted

KEY ITEMS OF CHRONOLOGY

Mexican independence	1821
Texas declared its independence from Mexico	1836
Harrison's administration	March 4–April 4,1841
Tyler's administration	April 4, 1841–1845
Departure of first wagon train	1841
Webster-Ashburton Treaty	1842
Texas formally annexed	December 1845
Polk's administration	1845–1849
Oregon Treaty	1846
Donner party	1846
Mexican War	1846–1848
Discovery of gold in California	1848

TERMS TO MASTER

Listed below are some important people or terms with which you should be familiar after your study of the chapter. Identify each name or term.

1. John Taylor
2. Webster-Ashburton Treaty
3. Manifest Destiny
4. Great Plains
5. *creole*
6. *mestizo*
7. Franciscans
8. Santa Fe Trail
9. Overland Trail
10. Donner Party
11. John Charles Frémont
12. Stephen F. Austin
13. Battle of the Alamo
14. Sam Houston
15. Santa Anna
16. Liberty party
17. "Fifty-four forty or fight"
18. Zachary Taylor
19. Stephan W. Kearny
20. Winfield Scott
21. Treaty of Guadalupe Hidalgo
22. James K. Polk

VOCABULARY BUILDING

Listed below are some words or phrases used in this chapter. Look in the dictionary for the meaning of each term you do not know.

1. retort
2. renegade
3. devoid
4. adherent
5. arid
6. contemptuous
7. thwart
8. presido
9. garrison
10. friar
11. diligence
12. proverbial
13. volatile
14. mongrel
15. cholera
16. maroon (v.)
17. covet
18. infidelity
19. qualm
20. dysentery

EXERCISES FOR UNDERSTANDING

When you have finished reading the chapter, answer each of the following questions. If you have difficulty, go back to the text and reread the section of the chapter related to the question.

Multiple-Choice Questions

Select the letter of the response that best completes the statement.

1. President John Tyler surprised and disappointed many because he
   A. was a Whig supporter of the "American System."
   B. was a Democratic advocate of national power.
   C. was a Whig defender of states' rights.
   D. deposed Clay as leader of the Whig party.

2. White expansion into the West threatened Indian culture by
   A. killing buffalo.
   B. converting Indians to Christianity.
   C. teaching Indians English.
   D. forcing Indians onto reservations.

3. The Overland Trail went from
   A. Missouri to Oregon.
   B. St. Louis to Sante Fe.
   C. Kansas to California via Colorado.
   D. Ohio across the prairie to Colorado.

4. The tragic fate of the Donner party involved
   A. slaughter by Indians.
   B. abduction and murder by Mexican authorities.
   C. cannibalism.
   D. confusion and death in the desert.

5. In the 1844 presidential election
   A. Henry Clay remained fully opposed to the annexation of Texas.
   B. Polk's expansionism attracted support from both the South and the West.
   C. Polk won a decisive mandate from both the popular and electoral votes.
   D. The Liberty party won a majority of the votes in New York.

6. The commander of Texan forces seeking independence was
   A. James K. Polk.
   B. Sam Houston.
   C. Stephen F. Austin.
   D. Zachary Taylor.

7. President Jackson delayed consideration of, and Van Buren shied away from, but Polk achieved
   A. the annexation of Texas.
   B. the destruction of the Bank of the United States.
   C. war with Mexico over California.
   D. the extension of slavery into the Northwest.

8. Opponents of the war with Mexico included
   A. New England abolitionists.
   B. a majority of the U.S. Congress.
   C. residents of Texas and California.
   D. proslavery leaders of the South.

9. Winfield Scott's major victory in the Mexican War came in
   A. California.
   B. Texas.
   C. Mexico.
   D. the Gulf of Mexico.

10. According to the Treaty of Guadalupe Hidalgo, the United States
    A. forfeited all claims above the 54° 40′ line.
    B. received $15 million from Mexico.
    C. gained California and New Mexico.
    D. prohibited slavery in Texas.

True-False Questions

Indicate whether each statement is true or false.

1. John Tyler was the first vice-president to succeed to the presidency upon the death of a president.

2. The slave trade was a major issue separating the United States and Britain in the 1840s.

3. Oregon Fever started in the 1840s.

4. Franciscan missions in California sought only to convert Indians to Catholicism.

5. Most of the western pioneers were recent European immigrants seeking a new start in America.

6. Western Indians responded to the pioneers' wagon trains with brutal assaults on the white settlers.

7. Sam Houston died at the Alamo.

8. The Spanish policy of granting hundreds of *ranchos* in California led the Mexican government to confiscate mission lands there and add them to the other *ranchos*.

9. The Mexican War involved the first major amphibious operation by United States forces.

10. In the Mexican War, far more soldiers died of disease than in combat.

Essay Questions

1. What were the major issues in national politics in the 1840s?

2. Describe the experience of traveling on the Overland Trail.

3. Compare and contrast the United States's acquisition of California and Oregon.

4. Why is James K. Polk often considered a successful president? Do you agree?

5. Did the United States have justification for entering a war with Mexico? Explain your answer, addressing any arguments for and against your position.

6. What were the effects of the Mexican War?

ANSWERS TO MULTIPLE-CHOICE
AND TRUE-FALSE QUESTIONS

Multiple-Choice Questions

1-C, 2-A, 3-A, 4-C, 5-B, 6-B, 7-A, 8-C, 9-A, 10-C

True-False Questions

1-T, 2-T, 3-T, 4-F, 5-F, 6-F, 7-F, 8-T, 9-T, 10-T

15 ∞

THE OLD SOUTH

CHAPTER OBJECTIVES

After you finish reading and studying this chapter, you should be able to

1. Describe the conditions that helped shape the antebellum South.

2. Separate reality from myth in descriptions of the antebellum South.

3. Analyze and explain the economic development of the antebellum South.

4. Understand the importance of honor in the culture of the Old South.

5. Describe and account for the different levels of white, black, and multiracial society in the antebellum South.

6. Understand the differences between the frontier South and the more established South.

7. Trace the development of the antislavery movement of the nation up to the early 1840s.

8. Explain some of the significant defenses of slavery developed in the South.

CHAPTER OUTLINE

    I. Myth and reality in the Old South
       A. Contrasting myths about southern whites
          1. Paternalistic and aristocratic
          2. Arrogant and brutal
       B. Distinctive features of the Old South
          1. Geography and weather

      2. Slavery
      3. Native-born population
      4. Other characteristics
      5. Assumption of distinctiveness
   C. Diverse farming
      1. King Cotton
      2. Food crops
      3. Soil exhaustion and erosion
   D. Manufacturing and trade
      1. Dependence on North
      2. Reasons for lack of industry
         a. Unsuitability of blacks
         b. Disdain of elites
         c. Profitability of slavery

II. White society in the South
   A. Tragedy of dependence on cotton
   B. Plantation
      1. Definition
      2. Extent of slaveholding
      3. Way of life
      4. Planters' wives
   C. Middle class
      1. Overseers
      2. Yeoman farmers
   D. "Poor whites"
      1. Different from yeomen
      2. "Lazy diseases"
   E. Culture of honor and violence
      1. Sense of honor
         a. Origins
         b. Role of women
         c. Manliness
      2. Violence
         a. Duels
         b. Anti-dueling societies
III. Black society in the South
   A. Free persons of color
      1. Origins and status
      2. Mulattoes
      3. Black slaveholders
      4. Occupations
      5. Discrimination against

B. Slavery
   1. Plantation slavery
      a. Work
      b. Owner's control
      c. Rebellion or flight
   2. Slave women
      a. Reproduction
      b. Demands of motherhood
      c. Work
      d. Sexual abuse
   3. Slave life
      a. Community
      b. Religion
      c. Family

IV. The Frontier South
   A. The Southwest
   B. Migration patterns
      1. To economic opportunity
      2. Young men
      3. Slaves
   C. Settlement
      1. Land purchases
      2. Environment
   D. Masculine culture
      1. Sex roles
      2. Drinking, gambling, fighting
   E. The example of Celia

V. Antislavery movements
   A. Efforts for colonization
      1. American Colonization Society, 1817
      2. Free black community's reactions to colonization
      3. Creation of Liberia
   B. Development of abolitionist movement
      1. From gradualism to abolitionism
         a. Garrison's *Liberator*
         b. Nat Turner's rebellion
         c. Antislavery groups
      2. Split in movement
         a. Radical wing
         b. Simple abolitionism
         c. Issue of women's rights
         d. New York anti-feminists

C. Black efforts against slavery
   1. Issue of involvement in white antislavery groups
   2. Former slaves as leading abolitionists
     a. Sojourner Truth's role
     b. Frederick Douglass's contributions
     c. Harriet Tubman
D. Nature of the Underground Railroad
E. Northern discrimination against blacks

VI. Reactions to antislavery agitation
  A. The "Gag Rule" in Congress
    1. Petitions to end slavery in District of Columbia
    2. House decision to table petitions
    3. John Quincy Adams's role
  B. Creation of the Liberty party (1840)
  C. Efforts to support slavery and deny abolitionism
    1. Biblical arguments for slavery
    2. Belief in intrinsic inferiority of blacks
    3. Socially impossible for blacks and whites to live together
    4. Attacks on northern wage slavery in the factory system
     a. Views of George Fitzhugh
     b. Calhoun's arguments
    5. Critics of slavery in the South silenced

KEY ITEMS OF CHRONOLOGY

African slave trade outlawed	1808
American Colonization Society founded	1817
William Lloyd Garrison published first issue of *The Liberator*	1831
Nat Turner insurrection	1831
American Anti-Slavery Society founded	1833
Liberty party founded	1840
Narrative of the Life of Frederick Douglass	1845

TERMS TO MASTER

Listed below are some important people or terms with which you should be familiar after your study of the chapter. Identify each name or term.

1. Old South
2. planter
3. yeoman farmer
4. "lazy diseases"
5. free blacks
6. Nat Turner
7. black belt
8. Old Southwest
9. Celia
10. abolitionism
11. gradual emancipation
12. American Colonization Society
13. William Lloyd Garrison
14. *The Liberator*
15. American Anti-Slavery Society
16. Grimké sisters
17. Frederick Douglass
18. Sojourner Truth
19. Underground Railroad
20. "gag rule"
21. Liberty Party
22. George Fitzhugh

VOCABULARY BUILDING

Listed below are some words or phrases used in this chapter. Look in the dictionary for the meaning of each term you do not know.

1. chivalric
2. penchant
3. disdain
4. preponderance
5. concubine
6. stereotype
7. forage
8. lethargy
9. malinger
10. camaraderie
11. impediment
12. truancy
13. manifestation
14. exhortation
15. kindling
16. miscegenation
17. anguish
18. pernicious
19. collaborate
20. intrepid

EXERCISES FOR UNDERSTANDING

When you have finished reading the chapter, answer each of the following questions. If you have difficulty, go back to the text and reread the section of the chapter related to the question.

Multiple-Choice Questions

Select the letter of the response that best completes the statement.

1. *Uncle Tom's Cabin* portrayed the Old South as a land of
   A. white-columned mansions occupied by paternalistic whites.
   B. arrogant, evil, aristocratic white planters.
   C. yeoman farmers who held Jeffersonian values.
   D. chivalry, honor, gallantry, and exalted women.

2. Between 1830 and 1860, the southern population experienced
   A. a growing concentration of wealth.
   B. more widespread ownership of slaves.
   C. declining prices for slaves and land.
   D. rapid industrialization.

3. In 1860 the percentage of southern whites who owned slaves was
   A. more than 50 percent.
   B. about 25 percent.
   C. 10 percent.
   D. less than 5 percent.

4. The emphasis on honor in the Old South involved
   A. dueling governed by strict rules.
   B. placing women on a pedestal.
   C. manliness and violence.
   D. all of the above

5. Preferred jobs for slaves included
   A. industrial workers.
   B. cotton field hands.
   C. tobacco field hands.
   D. skilled workers.

6. One difference between the Southwest and the Carolinas was that
   A. better land was available in the Carolinas and Virginia.
   B. the Southwest was much more isolated.
   C. the Southwest was healthier.
   D. the seaboard South offered more professional opportunities.

7. The split in the American Anti-Slavery Society in 1840 was over the issue of
   A. the colonization of freed blacks in Africa.
   B. the right of blacks to speak in racially mixed gatherings.
   C. the right of women to participate in the society.
   D. the role of blacks and women in the antislavery movement.

8. Before 1830 opponents of slavery wanted to
   A. compensate owners and free all slaves at one time.
   B. impose such a heavy tax on slaves that owners would want to get rid of them.
   C. send freed blacks back to Africa.
   D. ensure good treatment while keeping blacks enslaved.

9. Abolitionists did *not* include
   A. William Lloyd Garrison.
   B. Sarah Grimké.
   C. George Fitzhugh.
   D. Frederick Douglass.

10. The defenders of slavery
    A. did not want Congress even to consider petitions calling for the end of slavery in the District of Columbia.
    B. said that slavery was approved by the Bible.
    C. contended that slaves had better lives than northern industrial workers.
    D. used *all* of the above arguments.

True-False Questions

Indicate whether each statement is true or false.

1. Yeomen farmers made up the largest group of whites in the South, and most of them supported the institution of slavery.

2. The South's concentration on cotton meant few farmers had cows and pigs.

3. Planters (who each owned at least 20 slaves) owned more than half the South's slaves.

4. Free blacks could not live in the South.

5. In their religion, slaves could identify with the Israelites in Egypt.

6. In the Nat Turner rebellion, fifty-five whites died.

7. White southerners migrated to the Southwest because of the lack of good land in Alabama and Mississippi.

8. William Lloyd Garrison advocated colonization as a solution to the evil of slavery.

9. Harriet Tubman was a conductor on the Underground Railroad.

10. The "gag rule" restricted discussion of slavery among whites in the South.

Essay Questions

1. Was the Old South different from the other parts of the United States? Provide explanations in support of your answer.

2. Explain the diversity among the whites in the Old South.

3. Why did the South lack industrial development before the Civil War?

4. How did an emphasis on a code of honor affect the behavior of southern whites?

5. Discuss slavery in the antebellum South, including comment on the level of slaveholding, the typical life of plantation slaves, the diversity of the lives of slaves, and the profitability of slavery.

6. How did circumstances on the southwestern frontier differ from life in the Carolinas and Virginia? Which was preferable?

7. Describe the stages in the development of the antislavery movement and indicate the various factions that developed in the movement.

8. How did white southerners defend and justify slavery? Did their arguments make any sense?

ANSWERS TO MULTIPLE-CHOICE AND TRUE-FALSE QUESTIONS

Multiple-Choice Questions

1-B, 2-A, 3-D, 4-D, 5-D, 6-B, 7-C, 8-C, 9-C, 10-D

True-False Questions

1-T, 2-F, 3-T, 4-F, 5-T, 6-T, 7-F, 8-F, 9-T, 10-F

16 ∽

THE CRISIS OF UNION

CHAPTER OBJECTIVES

After you finish reading and studying this chapter, you should be able to

1. Explain the controversies that grew over the issue of slavery in the western lands acquired from Mexico.

2. List and explain the terms of the Compromise of 1850 and show to what extent those terms were fulfilled through 1861.

3. Account for the decline of the Whig party and the rise of the Republican party, noting the consequences of the change.

4. Explain the controversy over the Kansas-Nebraska Act and the resolution of that controversy.

5. Explain the meaning and importance of the Dred Scott decision.

6. Show how the election of 1860 demonstrated the breakup of political cohesion in the United States.

CHAPTER OUTLINE

I. Controversies over slavery in territories
   A. Conflict over Mexican War
      1. Wilmot Proviso
      2. Calhoun's response
      3. Extend Missouri Compromise
      4. Popular sovereignty

    B. Oregon as free territory

    C. Election of 1848

        1. Democrat Lewis Cass and popular sovereignty

        2. Whig Zachary Taylor

        3. Free Soil party

            a. Origin and support

            b. Van Buren and opposition to slavery

        4. Taylor's victory

    D. Question of California

        1. Gold

            a. Discovery in 1848

            b. Gold Rush

            c. Mining frontier

        2. Statehood

            a. Need for order

            b. President Taylor's position

            c. California and New Mexico organized as free states

 II. Compromise of 1850

    A. Development of the Compromise

        1. Clay's package of eight resolutions

        2. Calhoun's response

        3. Webster's plea for union

        4. Seward's response for the abolitionists

        5. Omnibus bill proposed by Committee of Thirteen

        6. Taylor's sudden death helps chances of compromise

        7. Fillmore supports Clay Compromise

        8. Douglas strategy of separate bills

        9. Terms of the compromise

    B. Reaction to the compromise

        1. Southern radicals keep slavery issue alive

        2. The Fugitive Slave Law

            a. Terms of the law

            b. Northern defiance of the law

        3. Gradual impact of *Uncle Tom's Cabin*

III. Election of 1852

    A. Democrats' choice of Pierce brings Van Burenites back into the party

    B. Whig choice of Winfield Scott alienates ethnic voters

    C. Election of Pierce fails to unify Democrats

IV. The expansion of Manifest Destiny

    A. Southern desire for Cuba

        1. Pierce's offer of purchase

        2. Revelation of the Ostend Manifesto

     B. Diplomatic gains in the Pacific
       1. Opening of China to U.S. trade encourages missionaries
       2. Perry's expedition helps open Japan to U.S. trade by 1858

  V. Kansas-Nebraska crisis
     A. Desire for a transcontinental railroad
     B. Davis's support for southern route leads to Gadsden Purchase
     C. The Kansas-Nebraska Act
       1. Douglas proposes popular sovereignty Nebraska bill
       2. Other concessions from Douglas
       3. Douglas's motives and the impact of the proposal
       4. Antislavery opposition
       5. Passage with support from Pierce

 VI. More weakening of the cords of union
     A. Northern defiance of Fugitive Slave Law
     B. Church organizations split over slavery
     C. Disintegration of the Whig party
       1. Emergence of American (Know-Nothing) party
       2. Other splinter parties
       3. Convergence into Republican party

 VII. The "battle" for Kansas
     A. Race for settlement by free-soilers and proslavery groups
     B. Establishment of a proslavery government
     C. The countergovernment in Topeka
     D. Violence in Lawrence, Pottawatomie, Ossawatomie, and elsewhere
     E. The Sumner-Butler-Brooks clash in the Senate

VIII. The election of 1856
     A. Remnants of American and Whig parties nominate Fillmore
     B. Republicans oppose slavery and nominate John C. Frémont
     C. Democrats choose Buchanan and appeal to ethnic voters
     D. Buchanan elected by only remaining national party

 IX. Buchanan faces three early crises as president
     A. Buchanan's prospects as a "doughface" president
     B. The Dred Scott decision
       1. Background to the case
       2. Analysis of the court's decision
       3. Reactions of North and South to the decision
     C. Continued conflict in Kansas
       1. Proslavery Lecompton Constitution
         a. Proslavery group adopts a constitution
         b. Buchanan supports the constitution
         c. Antislavery groups boycott the election
         d. Constitution with slavery wins

  2. Reaction of antislavery groups
     a. Acting governor convenes antislavery legislature
     b. Legislature calls for a second vote on constitution
     c. Constitution rejected
  3. Congress requires a third vote on the constitution
     a. Mechanics and basis for action
     b. Lecompton constitution again rejected
 D. Financial Panic of 1857
  1. Causes and nature of the panic
  2. Northern groups blame tariff increase
  3. Southerners gain new confidence for their system

X. The Lincoln-Douglas debates
 A. The Senate race of 1858 in Illinois
 B. The candidates described
 C. The Freeport Doctrine of Douglas
 D. Lincoln on the ropes
 E. Douglas elected

XI. John Brown's raid
 A. Brown's hopes for the raid
 B. Events of the raid
 C. Brown's trial and result
 D. Broader effects of the incident

XII. Election of 1860
 A. The Democratic party actions
  1. Convention's first phase of maneuvering
  2. Baltimore meeting nominates Douglas
 B. Breckinridge nominated by rump Democrats
 C. Republican party actions
  1. The emergence of Lincoln as nominee
  2. Appeals of the party platform
 D. Constitutional Union Party created to preserve the nation
 E. Nature of the campaign
 F. Explanation of Lincoln's election

XIII. Steps toward war
 A. Secession
  1. South Carolina leads
  2. Confederate government
  3. Basis for secession
 B. Buchanan's actions
  1. Belief in bluff of secession
  2. Refusal to be provocative
 C. Conflicts over Fort Sumter
 D. Failure of last efforts for compromise

KEY ITEMS OF CHRONOLOGY

Wilmot Proviso introduced	1846
Gold discovered in California	1848
Free Soil party started	1848
Death of Zachary Taylor	July 1850
Compromise of 1850	1850
Uncle Tom's Cabin	1852
Election of Franklin Pierce	1852
Commodore Matthew Perry arrived in Japan	1853
Gadsden Purchase	1853
Ostend Manifesto	1854
Kansas-Nebraska Act	1854
Creation of the Republican party	1854
Caning of Charles Sumner	May 22, 1856
Pottawatomie Massacre	May 24, 1856
Election of James Buchanan	1856
Dred Scott v. *Sandford*	1857
Financial panic	1857
Lincoln-Douglas debates	1858
John Brown's raid at Harper's Ferry	1859
Secession of South Carolina	December 20, 1860
Confederate State of America organized and Jefferson Davis inaugurated president of the Confederacy	February 1861
Lincoln's inauguration	March 4, 1861

TERMS TO MASTER

Listed below are some important people or terms with which you should be familiar after your study of the chapter. Identify each name or term.

1. Wilmot Proviso
2. popular sovereignty
3. Free Soil party
4. "conscience" Whigs and "cotton" Whigs
5. Compromise of 1850
6. Henry Clay
7. Stephen A. Douglas
8. fire eaters
9. Fugitive Slave Act of 1850
10. *Uncle Tom's Cabin*
11. Ostend Manifesto
12. Gadsden Purchase
13. Republican party
14. "bleeding" Kansas
15. John Brown
16. Pottawatomie Massacre
17. Charles Sumner
18. Kansas-Nebraska Act
19. Roger Taney
20. *Dred Scott* v. *Sandford*
21. Lecompton Constitution

22. Freeport Doctrine
23. Harper's Ferry, Virginia
24. John C. Breckinridge
25. Abraham Lincoln

26. John Bell
27. Ordinance of Secession
28. Jefferson Davis
29. Crittenden Compromise

VOCABULARY BUILDING

Listed below are some words or phrases used in this chapter. Look in the dictionary for the meaning of each term you do not know.

1. dogma
2. converge
3. scurvy
4. burgeoning
5. forthright
6. implacable
7. omnibus
8. stealth
9. escapade
10. repudiate

11. lackluster
12. pliable
13. diversion
14. poignant
15. scoundrel
16. psychosomatic
17. bulwark
18. sinewy
19. bushwhacking
20. martyr

EXERCISES FOR UNDERSTANDING

When you have finished reading the chapter, answer each of the following questions. If you have difficulty, go back to the text and reread the section of the chapter related to the question.

Multiple-Choice Questions

Select the letter of the response that best completes the statement.

1. Lewis Cass's idea of popular sovereignty called for
   A. the citizens of a territory to decide the fate of slavery in that territory.
   B. a national referendum on controversial issues such as the tariff, slavery, and the national bank.
   C. electing presidents by popular vote without an electoral college.
   D. giving blacks, including slaves, the right to vote in national elections.

2. The mining communities in the West were unusual in that they
   A. were extremely unstable and disorderly.
   B. contained a high percentage of women.
   C. were ethnically quite homogeneous.
   D. all of the above

3. The creator of the Compromise of 1850 was
   A. Daniel Webster.
   B. David Wilmot.
   C. Stephen A. Douglas.
   D. Henry Clay.

4. Succeeding Zachary Taylor as president in 1850, New York's Millard Fillmore
   A. sided with the antislavery forces.
   B. was strongly proslavery.
   C. avoided taking a stand on slavery in the territories.
   D. none of the above

5. A "northern man with southern principles" described President
   A. Abraham Lincoln.
   B. Zachary Taylor.
   C. Franklin Pierce.
   D. James Buchanan.

6. The Pottawatomie Massacre occurred in
   A. California.
   B. Kansas.
   C. Nebraska.
   D. Missouri.

7. The failure of Kansas to gain statehood before the Civil War can be attributed to
   A. the fervent desire of many to run a transcontinental railroad through the area.
   B. the controversy and violence surrounding the effort to push through a proslavery constitution.
   C. the political ambitions of Abraham Lincoln, who worked to keep the area a territory.
   D. the success of proslavery forces in their slaughter of innocent citizens.

8. The Dred Scott decision of the United States Supreme Court involved
   A. a slave who had been taken to live in Kansas.
   B. a slave suing for his freedom because his master had taken him into free territory.
   C. a former slave who sued for his wife's freedom on the grounds that she had been married to a free black.
   D. a slave who had been freed by his master and who challenged the Fugitive Slave Act of 1850.

9. The Lecompton Constitution of 1857
   A. made Kansas a slave state.
   B. approved popular sovereignty in the territories.
   C. permitted Missouri to vote for or against slavery.
   D. united Democrats behind the idea of "free soil."

10. The efforts to preserve the Union in 1861 included
    A. an agreement to postpone the inauguration of Lincoln so that Breckinridge could be made president.
    B. the proposal of a constitutional amendment to guarantee protection for slavery everywhere it then existed.
    C. a plan to withdraw federal troops from all military installations in the South.
    D. passage of a law to outlaw slavery in all northern states.

True-False Questions

Indicate whether each statement is true or false.

1. The Wilmot Proviso proposed to forbid slavery in any territory acquired during the Mexican War.

2. "Free soil, free speech, free labor, and free men" was the slogan of Cotton Whigs.

3. As a result of the Compromise of 1850, California entered the union without any reference to slavery.

4. The Fugitive Slave Law actually worked to strengthen antislavery forces in the North.

5. The successful opening of trade to Asia helped to support demand for a transcontinental railroad.

6. Harriet Beecher Stowe's book was a commercial failure.

7. Most Kansas settlers came from New England.

8. As an immediate result of the Lincoln-Douglas debate, Lincoln was elected president.

9. Lincoln was president when seven southern states voted to secede from the Union.

10. In 1859 John Brown was captured at Harper's Ferry, Virginia.

Essay Questions

1. What was the Compromise of 1850 and how did it settle the slavery issue?

2. Why did diplomatic efforts of the United States in the 1850s often fail to turn attention away from sectional differences and slavery? Which diplomatic successes did not bring sectional repercussions?

3. What did the Supreme Court decide in *Dred Scott* v. *Sandford*? Why was it an important case?

4. How did the political parties change in the 1840s and 1850s?

5. What attempts to solve the growing sectional crisis did Presidents Taylor, Fillmore, Pierce, and Buchanan make? Why did each fail?

6. Describe the political differences between Abraham Lincoln and Stephen A. Douglas in 1858 and 1860.

ANSWERS TO MULTIPLE-CHOICE AND TRUE-FALSE QUESTIONS

Multiple-Choice Questions

1-A, 2-A, 3-D, 4-D, 5-C, 6-B, 7-B, 8-B, 9-A, 10-B

True-False Questions

1-T, 2-F, 3-F, 4-T, 5-T, 6-F, 7-F, 8-F, 9-F, 10-T

17 ∞

THE WAR OF THE UNION

CHAPTER OBJECTIVES

After you finish reading and studying this chapter, you should be able to

1. Explain how the outbreak of fighting occurred.

2. Analyze the advantages that each side had in the war.

3. Describe the problems associated with raising an army for both the North and the South.

4. Trace the major strategic and military developments of the Civil War.

5. Explain the political problems of the governments in both the North and the South.

6. Account for the emancipation of slaves and describe its impact.

7. Describe Confederate diplomatic aspirations.

8. Explain how each side financed the war and the economic effects of the war on the North.

CHAPTER OUTLINE

  I. The start of war
    A. Lincoln
      1. Trip to Washington
      2. "Union is perpetual"
    B. The South
      1. Secession
      2. Firing on Fort Sumter

      3. Union blockade

      4. Secession of upper South

      5. Border state choices

      6. Southern unionists

  C. Advantages of each side

      1. The North

         a. Population

         b. Industry

         c. Farm production

         d. Transportation

      2. The South

         a. Geography

         b. Defensive war

         c. Strong military tradition

  D. First Battle of Bull Run

      1. Caused by naive optimism

      2. Northern retreat

II. Early course of the war

  A. Strategies

      1. Union's three-pronged plan

         a. Defend Washington and pressure Richmond

         b. Blockade South

         c. Divide Confederacy

      2. Confederate strategy

         a. Force stalemate

         b. Foreign support

         c. Negotiated settlement

  B. Naval action

      1. Ironclads

      2. Union successes in South

  C. Raising armies

      1. Enlistments

      2. Conscription

      3. Opposition to draft

  D. Activity in West

      1. Continued settlement

      2. Fighting in Kansas

      3. Indian involvement

      4. U. S. Grant

         a. Unconditional surrender in Tennessee

         b. Costly loss at Shiloh

  E. McClellan's campaign in East

      1. McClellan's character

2. Lincoln's demands
3. Advance on Richmond
4. Lee given command in the South
5. Lee's attack on McClellan
6. Halleck replaces McClellan
   a. Confederate trap
   b. Union defeat
  G. Battle of Antietam
   1. McClellan's hesitancy
   2. Failure of Lee's invasion
  H. Fredericksburg
   1. Union attack
   2. Burnside withdraws

III. Emancipation and blacks
  A. War's effects on emancipation
  B. Lincoln's considerations
  C. The proclamation
  D. Reactions to emancipation
  E. Blacks in the military
  F. Thirteenth Amendment

IV. Women and the Civil War
  A. Nurses
   1. Clara Barton
   2. Sally Tompkins
  B. New responsibilities
  C. Widows and spinsters

V. Wartime government
  A. Power in Union shifts to North
   1. Protective tariff
   2. Transcontinental railroad
   3. Homestead Act
   4. Other legislation
  B. Financing the war
   1. Union's revenues
    a. Greenbacks
    b. Bonds
    c. Capital accumulation
   2. Confederate problems
  C. Confederate diplomacy
   1. Attempts at recognition
   2. Success in obtaining supplies

D. Wartime politics
   1. Union
      a. Pressure of the Radicals
      b. Divided Democrats
      c. Suspension of habeas corpus
      d. Elections of 1862 and 1864
   2. Confederate
      a. Discontent in South
      b. Problems of states' rights

VI. The faltering Confederacy in 1863
  A. Hooker leads the Union
  B. Chancellorsville
    1. Peak of Lee's career
    2. Loss of Stonewall Jackson
  C. Union wins at Vicksburg and Gettysburg
    1. Grant's siege of Vicksburg
    2. Gettysburg
      a. Lee's invasion
      b. Pickett's charge
      c. Confederate defeat
      d. Cemetery
    3. Confederate surrender of Vicksburg
  D. Chattanooga
    1. Confederate advantage
    2. Federal victory

VII. Defeat of the Confederacy
  A. Situation at end of 1863
    1. Confederate morale
    2. Grant's plan to attack
  B. War of extermination
    1. Grant pursues Lee in Virginia
    2. Sherman marches across Georgia
  C. Surrender at Appomattox

VIII. The aftermath of the war

KEY ITEMS OF CHRONOLOGY

Lincoln's inauguration	March 4, 1861
Guns fire on Fort Sumter	4:30 A.M., April 12, 1861
First Battle of Bull Run	July 1861
Monitor v. *Merrimack*	March 1862

Battle of Shiloh	April 1862
Second Battle of Bull Run	August 1862
Battle of Antietam	September 1862
Battle of Fredericksburg	December 1862
Emancipation Proclamation (Preliminary, September 1862)	January 1, 1863
Battle of Chancellorsville	May 1863
Victories at Vicksburg and Gettysburg	July 4, 1863
Battle of the Wilderness	May 1864
Lincoln reelected	November 1864
Destruction of Atlanta	November 1864
Surrender at Appomattox	April 9, 1865 (Palm Sunday)

TERMS TO MASTER

Listed below are some important people or terms with which you should be familiar after your study of the chapter. Identify each name or term.

1. writ of habeas corpus
2. Robert E. Lee
3. Battle of Bull Run
4. *Merrimack* and *Monitor*
5. Battle of Shiloh
6. Jefferson Davis
7. Eastern and Western Theaters
8. George B. McClellan
9. Ulysses S. Grant
10. Antietam
11. Fredericksburg
12. Emancipation Proclamation
13. Clara Barton
14. greenbacks
15. Copperheads
16. Vicksburg
17. Gettysburg
18. William T. Sherman
19. Battle of Chattanooga
20. Appomattox Court House

VOCABULARY BUILDING

Listed below are some words or phrases used in this chapter. Look in the dictionary for the meaning of each term you do not know.

1. bolster
2. epitomize
3. impetuous
4. entwine
5. pell-mell
6. furlough
7. flout
8. proximity
9. plateau
10. annihilate
11. dithering
12. carnage
13. exasperate
14. embark

15. demoralize
16. insubordination
17. adversary

18. moratorium
19. consummate
20. pugnacity

EXERCISES FOR UNDERSTANDING

When you have finished reading the chapter, answer each of the following questions. If you have difficulty, go back to the text and reread the section of the chapter related to the question.

Multiple-Choice Questions

Select the letter of the response that best completes the statement.

1. Southern advantages in the Civil War included the region's
   A. greater farm production.
   B. superior transportation.
   C. defensive position.
   D. larger and stronger navy.

2. The Union army contained
   A. 100,000 southerners.
   B. 200,000 black troops.
   C. units organized along ethnic lines (Irish, German, etc.).
   D. all of the above

3. From July 1861 to May 1862, military action in the East primarily involved
   A. fighting for control of Washington, D.C.
   B. naval forces.
   C. struggles for control of the Shenandoah Valley.
   D. battles for control of border areas such as Maryland.

4. A draft to raise an army
   A. encountered opposition in both the North and South.
   B. was not necessary in the Confederacy.
   C. provided most of the men for the Union army.
   D. was left entirely up to the individual states in the South.

5. In issuing the Emancipation Proclamation, Lincoln
   A. fulfilled his long-held objective of freeing the slaves.
   B. ended slavery throughout the United States.
   C. yielded to wartime necessity.
   D. hoped to end problems with fugitive slaves.

6. During the Civil War the United States Congress
   A. could do little because of the absent southern representatives.
   B. neglected legislation not directly related to the war due to a lack of funds.
   C. played a major role in choosing and firing generals to lead the Union forces.
   D. adopted a tariff, a homestead law, and a law providing for a transcontinental railroad.

7. The North financed the war with all the following except
   A. excise taxes and bonds.
   B. higher tariffs.
   C. printing more money.
   D. property taxes.

8. Three major Union victories in 1863 were
   A. Chancellorsville, Fredericksburg, and Gettysburg.
   B. Chattanooga, Gettysburg, and Vicksburg.
   C. Antietam, Chancellorsville, and Gettysburg.
   D. Antietam, Gettysburg, and Vicksburg.

9. The Union march through Georgia, including the destruction of Atlanta, was led by
   A. Ulysses S. Grant.
   B. George B. McClellan.
   C. P. G. T. Beauregard.
   D. William Tecumseh Sherman.

10. In the course of the Civil War
    A. more men were killed or died of disease than in all other American wars combined.
    B. 50 percent of all males served in the war.
    C. few civilians were affected by the fighting that occurred.
    D. women were permitted to serve in combat units only on the northern side.

True-False Questions

Indicate whether each statement is true or false.

1. All states with slaves joined the Confederacy.

2. The first shots of the Civil War were fired at Bull Run.

3. Union forces won both battles at Bull Run.

4. The bloodiest single day of the Civil War occurred in the Battle of Antietam.

5. Lincoln had great difficulty finding effective military commanders.

6. Blacks provided about 10 percent of the Union Army forces.

7. Clara Barton served as the superintendent of Women Nurses for the Confederacy.

8. Northerners who wanted a negotiated end to the Civil War were called Copperheads.

9. Stonewall Jackson was a pioneer in the practice of total war.

10. Lincoln made William Sherman general-in-chief in 1864.

Essay Questions

1. Which side seemed to have the major advantages at the opening of the war? Did the apparent advantages have a major effect on the war's outcome?

2. Did the Union or the Confederacy have greater problems raising an army and financing the war? Explain.

3. In what ways was the Civil War a "modern" war?

4. Why did President Lincoln issue the Emancipation Proclamation? What were its effects?

5. Which was more significant to the result of the war: military action in the East or the West? Explain the differences.

6. From a military standpoint, what were the turning points in the Civil War?

ANSWERS TO MULTIPLE-CHOICE AND TRUE-FALSE QUESTIONS

Multiple-Choice Questions

1-C, 2-D, 3-B, 4-A, 5-C, 6-D, 7-D, 8-B, 9-D, 10-A

True-False Questions

1-F, 2-T, 3-F, 4-T, 5-T, 6-T, 7-F, 8-T, 9-F, 10-F

18 ⌘

RECONSTRUCTION:
NORTH AND SOUTH

CHAPTER OBJECTIVES

After you finish reading and studying this chapter, you should be able to

1. Assess the impact of the Civil War on both the North and South the and on the status of freed blacks.

2. Outline the circumstances that led to Radical Reconstruction.

3. Describe the nature and extent of Radical Reconstruction.

4. Explain the process that returned control of the South to the conservatives.

5. Evaluate the contributions and failures of the Grant administration.

6. Understand the outcome of the election of 1876, the effects of that election, and the special arrangements made to conclude it.

7. Appraise the overall impact of Reconstruction.

CHAPTER OUTLINE

I. The war's aftermath
  A. The North
    1. Friendly to business
    2. National power centralized
      a. Morrill Tariff
      b. National Banking Act
      c. Transcontinental railroad
      d. Homestead Act
      e. Morrill Land Grant Act

B. The South
   1. Property destroyed
   2. Worthless money and bonds
   3. Slaves freed
   4. Relationships transformed
   5. Confederates embittered
C. The freed slaves
   1. New status
      a. Legal rights
      b. Lack of property
   2. Freedmen's Bureau
      a. Help freedmen
      b. Limited powers

II. Battle over Reconstruction
   A. Lincoln's plan
      1. Provisions
      2. Implementation
   B. Congressional reaction
      1. Radical critics
      2. Wade-Davis Bill
      3. Lincoln's response
   C. Assassination of Lincoln
   D. Johnson's plan
      1. Johnson's background
         a. Tennessee
         b. Jacksonian
         c. Unionist
         d. Election
      2. Ideas on Union
         a. Indestructible
         b. No Reconstruction
      3. Similar to Lincoln's plan
   E. Southern resistance
      1. Elects ex-Confederates
      2. "Black codes"
   F. Congressional Radicals
      1. Joint Committee on Reconstruction
         a. Role of Radicals
         b. Thaddeus Stevens
      2. Motivation
         a. Humanitarianism
         b. Bitterness
         c. Black vote

        3. Constitutional theory
   G. Johnson vs. Congress
        1. Veto of Freedmen's Bureau extension
        2. Johnson attacks Radicals
        3. Veto of Civil Rights Act overridden
        4. The Fourteenth Amendment

III. Congressional Reconstruction
   A. Elections of 1866
   B. Legislation
        1. Military Reconstruction Act
        2. Command of the Army Act
        3. Tenure of Office Act
        4. Limits on Supreme Court review
   C. Impeachment and trial of Johnson
        1. Mutual hostility
        2. Initial effort failed
        3. Violation of Tenure in Office Act
        4. Political purposes
        5. Trial
        6. Role of Edmund Ross
        7. Effects of trial
   D. Republican rule in South
        1. Readmission of states
        2. Role of Union League

IV. The reconstructed South
   A. Attitudes of whites
   B. The life of freedmen
        1. Military experience
        2. Independent organizations
        3. Families reaffirmed
        4. Farm workers
           a. Wage laborers
           b. Tenant farmers
        5. Schools
   C. Black political life
        1. Illiterate and inexperienced
        2. Increasing participation
        3. Divisions among blacks
        4. Limited political role
   D. White Republicans in South
        1. Carpetbaggers
        2. Scalawags
   E. The Radicals' record

    F. White terror
       1. Ku Klux Klan
       2. Enforcement Acts
    G. Conservative resurgence
       1. Weakened morale
       2. Mobilized white vote
       3. Decline of northern concern

V. The Grant years
    A. The election of 1868
       1. Reasons for support of Grant
       2. The Grant ticket and platform
       3. Democratic programs and candidates
       4. Results
       5. The character of Grant's leadership
    B. Proposal to pay the government debt
    C. Scandals
       1. Jay Gould's effort to corner the gold market
       2. The Crédit-Mobilier exposure
       3. Secretary of War and the Indian Bureau
       4. "Whiskey Ring"
       5. Grant's personal role in the scandals
    D. Reform and the election of 1872
       1. Liberal Republicans nominate Greeley in 1872
       2. Grant's advantages
    E. Economic panic
       1. Causes for the depression
       2. Severity of the depression
       3. Democratic control of the House in 1874
       4. Reissue of greenbacks
       5. Resumption of specie payments approved in 1875

VI. The Compromise of 1877
    A. Election of 1876
       1. Republicans nominate Hayes
       2. Democrats run Tilden
       3. Parties' stances
       4. Uncertain results
    B. Electoral Commission
    C. Compromises
    D. End of Reconstruction

KEY ITEMS OF CHRONOLOGY

Lincoln's plan for Reconstruction announced	1863
Wade-Davis Bill	1864
Joint Committee on Reconstruction established	1865
Thirteenth Amendment ratified	1865
Creation of Freedmen's Bureau	1865
Assassination of Lincoln	April 14, 1865
Johnson's plan for Reconstruction announced	May 29, 1865
Veto of Freedmen's Bureau Extension Bill	February 1866
Congress overrode Johnson's veto of Civil Rights Act	April 1866
Fourteenth Amendment passed by Congress	June 1866
Ku Klux Klan organized in the South	1866
Military Reconstruction Act	March 2, 1867
Johnson replaces Stanton with Grant as secretary of war	August 1867
House votes to impeach Johnson	February 1868
Trial of Johnson in Senate	March 5 to May 26, 1868
Fourteenth Amendment ratified	1868
All southern states except Mississippi, Texas, and Virginia, readmitted to Congress	June 1868
Texas v. *White* decision of Supreme Court	1868
Grant administrations	1869–1877
Mississippi, Texas, and Virginia readmitted to Congress	1870
Fifteenth Amendment ratified	1870
Resumption Act	1875
Hayes elected	1876–1877
End of Reconstruction	1877

TERMS TO MASTER

Listed below are some important people or terms with which you should be familiar after your study of the chapter. Identify each name or term.

1. Freedmen's Bureau
2. Wade-Davis Bill
3. pocket veto
4. "iron clad" oath
5. Black Codes
6. John Wilkes Booth
7. Radical Republicans
8. Andrew Johnson
9. Thaddeus Stevens
10. Charles Sumner
11. Fourteenth Amendment
12. Military Reconstruction Act
13. Command of the Army Act
14. Tenure of Office Act

15. carpetbaggers and scalawags
16. Ku Klux Klan
17. Ulysses S. Grant
18. hard and soft money
19. Liberal Republicans

20. Jay Gould
21. Crédit-Mobilier
22. Rutherford B. Hayes
23. Samuel J. Tilden
24. Compromise of 1877

VOCABULARY BUILDING

Listed below are some words or phrases used in this chapter. Look in the dictionary for the meaning of each term you do not know.

1. levee
2. anarchy
3. intransigence
4. affiliation
5. indulgence
6. impenitence
7. petulant
8. perversity
9. inversion
10. immunity

11. boor
12. dilute
13. tedious
14. impeach
15. harangue
16. resilience
17. lenient
18. castigate
19. factious
20. cormorant

EXERCISES FOR UNDERSTANDING

When you have finished reading the chapter, answer each of the following questions. If you have difficulty, go back to the text and reread the section of the chapter related to the question.

Multiple-Choice Questions

Select the letter of the response that best completes the statement.

1. The Wade-Davis Bill reflected the reconstruction ideas of
   A. southerners.
   B. Abraham Lincoln.
   C. Andrew Johnson.
   D. Radical Republicans.

2. After emancipation, the freed slaves received
   A. forty acres of land under the Confiscation Act.
   B. individual homesteads under the Morrill Land Grant Act.
   C. the right to vote under the Fourteenth Amendment.
   D. help with labor contracts from the Freedmen's Bureau.

3. The Reconstruction policies of the Radical Republicans were probably motivated by
   A. a humanitarian concern for the former slaves.
   B. hopes for Republican power in the South.
   C. bitterness over having to fight the costly war.
   D. all of the above

4. Before becoming president, Andrew Johnson had been
   A. a Democrat.
   B. an abolitionist.
   C. a senator from Maine.
   D. all of the above

5. Andrew Johnson's plan to restore the Union
   A. closely resembled Lincoln's.
   B. was quite similar to the Radicals' program.
   C. involved total reconstruction of the South.
   D. did not include any black suffrage.

6. The Radical southern governments during Reconstruction
   A. were unusually honest and moral.
   B. operated frugally and did not go into debt.
   C. refused to aid private corporations such as railroads.
   D. gave unusual attention to education and poor relief.

7. As a result of his impeachment, President Andrew Johnson
   A. was removed from office.
   B. gained the upper hand in his fight with Congress over Reconstruction.
   C. lost considerable power and influence.
   D. decided to leave politics.

8. States were prohibited from denying freedmen the right to vote by the
   A. Thirteenth Amendment.
   B. Fourteenth Amendment.
   C. Fifteenth Amendment.
   D. Military Reconstruction Act.

9. U. S. Grant was guilty of
   A. refusing to turn documents over to Congress for its investigation.
   B. trying to block the implementation of Reconstruction laws.
   C. choosing his appointees unwisely.
   D. taking funds from the federal treasury.

10. Reconstruction came to an end in
    A. 1870.
    B. 1877.
    C. 1888.
    D. 1890.

True-False Questions

Indicate whether each statement is true or false.

1. After the Civil War, many Confederates left the South.

2. The Black Codes were laws enacted by southern legislatures that were controlled by the former slaves.

3. To retain political power, Radical Republicans had to disfranchise black and white southerners.

4. Congress generally accepted the "forfeited rights theory" in explaining secession.

5. During "Black Reconstruction," blacks controlled most southern state governments.

6. Scalawags were white, southern-born Republicans.

7. In 1868, President Johnson avoided being removed from office by one vote.

8. Farmers usually advocated "hard" money.

9. The Crédit-Mobilier was involved in trading greenbacks to France for gold.

10. The Compromise of 1877 included a southerner as Speaker of the House.

Essay Questions

1. Did the Civil War have a greater impact on the North or the South? Explain.

2. How did the Reconstruction plans of Lincoln, Johnson, and the Radicals differ? Which was the best? Why?

3. Radical Reconstruction was not imposed until two years after the end of the Civil War and drew bitter opposition from the whites in the South. Would it have been better accepted if it had been imposed in May 1865 instead of March 1867? Explain why or why not.

4. Was either Grant or Johnson a successful president? Who was the more successful? How?

5. Why was Andrew Johnson impeached? What was the outcome?

6. What were the major provisions of the Fourteenth Amendment?

7. Explain the provisions of the Compromise of 1877 and its effects on the South.

ANSWERS TO MULTIPLE-CHOICE
AND TRUE-FALSE QUESTIONS

Multiple-Choice Questions

1-D, 2-D, 3-D, 4-A, 5-A, 6-D, 7-C, 8-C, 9-C, 10-B

True-False Questions

1-F, 2-F, 3-F, 4-T, 5-F, 6-T, 7-T, 8-F, 9-F, 10-F